ORGANIC VEGETABLE GARDENING 101

A BEGINNER GARDENING GUIDE WITH TIPS ON HOW TO GROW VEGETABLES

BY CLAY WATTS
WWW.CLAYWATTSBOOKS.COM

CONTENTS

"A garden feeds more than the table; it feeds the soul."

— UNKNOWN

A SPECIAL GIFT TO OUR READERS

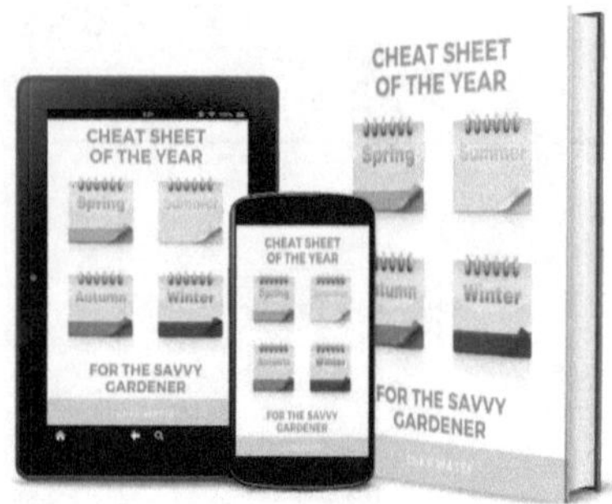

Included with your purchase of this book is our Cheat Sheet of the Year for The Savvy Gardener. In this cheat sheet, you'll have a list of a few tricks, tips, and reminders to do every month of the year to start or maintain your garden.

Scan the QR code below and let us know what email address to deliver it to.

INTRODUCTION

Here's a perplexing fact: healthy foods are more expensive than unhealthy foods. Harvard School of Public Health found that you are more likely to spend about $1.50 a day buying healthy foods than to go all out for processed foods. But it comes with its perks. What am I talking about?

When you really look at it, the $1.50 you spend on healthy foods is more like a health insurance fee. You are protecting your future self from the myriad health issues that **WILL** arise when you live and breathe junk foods. That's great, isn't it? But here comes a pain in the you-know-where.

There are a lot of problems associated with buying healthy foods. Just because they are healthy doesn't mean they can't pose a risk to your health.

There are fertilizers. Yes, shops have to use these to churn out more quantity. I mean, they have to be in business, right? Do you think apples grow all year? Yet, somehow, you find them every single day in stores near you.

What about pesticides in the soil? Now, there is no way for you to know what was used to treat the soil in which the foods were grown. So, what do you do?

I am sure you are familiar with all of these issues, but here is something interesting.

Did you know that some foods believed to be healthy are actually junk food in disguise? Yep! Ever gone to a restaurant and felt that ordering salad would make your meal healthier? I mean, salad combines different natural foods, one of which is veggies. But here's one thing you might not know: most restaurants actually dish out unhealthy salad dressings unknown to you. This "healthy" meal is loaded with sugar, vegetable oil, trans fat, and, worst of all, artificial chemicals! Think about this: why did the salad dressing you eat on a date night in some fancy restaurant taste better than the one you prepare at home?

It doesn't end there.

We have other cases like that of whole wheat grains, which are not usually made from whole wheat. The pulverized grains actually raise our blood sugar levels. Yes, you read that right.

The alternative to all of this is **GROWING YOUR FOOD**. Of course, it's not like it's the simplest of options, but it is the best decision you will make.

Growing your food leads to:

- Eating more nutritious foods—no fertilizers or unhealthy food disguised as healthy.
- Staying physically active. Consider all the hours you will spend nurturing your garden.
- Getting more doses of vitamin D. Who says only your plants get to enjoy all the sun rays? Now, that would have been unfair, wouldn't it? Fortunately, you get to enjoy its benefits also!
- Most importantly, you get to save money. Yes, growing your food is ten times cheaper than buying it.

I understand that you might feel like it's hard to grow food where you live, with seasonal changes and all that. What if summer in your region lasts for a couple of weeks instead of months? Worse yet, what if you don't have enough space in your garden to grow food? And what if your home doesn't get enough sunlight? I get it. The process can be overwhelming. I mean, just thinking about it already is. Now, imagine actually trying to nurture a garden. That would be *overwhelming 2.0.*

Like me, I get that you want to feel more empowered in your food ownership. You want to own it! You want to be able to go off-grid a bit more; you love the idea of being in control of your food source.

There is a long list of issues surrounding growing your food. But right now, I want you to take a step back from all of that and think about this instead.

You can have a flourishing garden. Yes, I said it. Despite the myths you must have heard about what it takes to own and nurture a garden, growing your food is possible and less tricky if you know EXACTLY what and what not to do.

So, what do you need to do?

Firstly, you need to know the difference between a good spot and *the perfect* spot for your garden. A bit confusing, right? Well, let me break it down for you. Yes, you might have a space that's fit for a garden, but the soil there might not be fertile enough to set up a garden. This makes it a lot harder to set up your garden, but it isn't that complex. You can grow the perfect plant right in your backyard on that soil that you think is not so fertile. Yep! And it's way easier than you imagine.

You might say, "But I have a backyard filled with rocks! How do I go about it?" And I will tell you again, you can create the perfect garden with the most potent soil!

Of course, that's not all there is to it. There is also planning to consider, something called companion gardening, covering, and mixing it all up. I could go on listing ideas, but it will only overwhelm you. And we are trying to stay away from that, right?

So, what about the things you shouldn't do?

Sometimes, we forget we have to deal with weeds, which could single-handedly ruin that beautiful garden of yours. Beginner gardeners also tend to try and grow every kind of vegetable at once to have it all. That's a problem. You can't do that.

Does it end there? Of course not!

This is where my book comes in.

This book takes you from a place of little to no knowledge about gardening to the cultivation of your first crop. It details the steps on how best to grow your vegetables. It won't just show you where to get started, what to focus on, what you shouldn't do, and how to grow the best crops. The idea is to take you through everything step by step using simple language.

Don't worry—I don't intend to take you through biology or agriculture class. I wouldn't be able to write this book if my parents had taught me that way.

Besides, growing up watching my parents nurture their garden made it easy for me to learn everything I could. I saw how my mom planted crops, nurtured them, and eventually harvested these veggies with ease. She made it look so easy. You could say it came down to her years of experience, but we had our ups and downs.

Like those times when it would rain so heavily that it wouldn't only wither the plants but also kill their roots. Or those times when we had to spend more than we bargained for because we initially overlooked some maintenance. As a kid, I would sometimes water a crop too much. My mother would then hold my hand as I held on to the water can saying, "There you go, Clay. This is how you do it." Of course, I didn't get it right away (ha-ha), but I got the hang of it.

With every complication we faced, we learned and avoided a similar scenario. This made me develop a relationship with plants at a tender age. I was probably just seven or eight. I could somehow sense their needs and desires in a unique way that benefited everyone involved. Of course, I had my parents to thank for that.

So, here I am, sharing what my mother's genius taught me and how I lived surrounded by a garden in my home.

Honestly, it starts with having a passion. I know this. However, over time, you won't need your passion to fuel your actions. But it will be there, as seeing your garden blossom is a delightful and beautiful sight—well, that's if you do it properly.

Now, why don't we get started on how you can properly build and nurture your organic vegetable garden?

1

WHY YOU SHOULD ALWAYS BE GROWING YOUR FOOD

A CRASH HISTORY OF AGRICULTURE (DON'T WORRY, THERE WON'T BE ANYTHING LIKE CARICA PAPAYA.)

In the beginning, there were trees, veggies, lettuce, lemons, crispy fruits, dates, palms, strawberries, avocados, and all other types of fruits you could ever imagine. During this period, men were happy-go-lucky, strategic hunters and gatherers, always going around picking up dates and shooting some wild turkey *(let's assume that it existed back then)* for dinner.

This went on for centuries and maybe millennia, but, at some point, men decided to stop roaming around for wild bears and dates. He came up with the idea of having a home and growing all he wanted—revolutionary, right? Hell yes!

He built his first house – a fancy bungalow hut. Then he began working on a piece of land where he tended his own food and nurtured his own farm animals. This revolutionary idea became known as agriculture—what we all tie our hunger pangs to. Imagine if man hadn't achieved that idea. Then you would probably have to travel to Missouri or Pennsylvania for lunch and Massachusetts for dinner. But thanks to those early farmers, you can go to your garden instead, cut some veggies, and turn them into a portion of yummy food.

However, over the years, agriculture has grown from the footprint of early men, which was basically organic materials for growing plants, into a more complex form. This means that instead of using animal dung (manure) to treat the soil into having more nutrients, man has now created an alternative nutrient supplement to make the soil more potent, which was also quite revolutionary. This alternative is called a fertilizer[1], and it falls into the non-organic farming[2] category.

In non-organic farming, synthetic chemicals are used to boost plant growth and development. Examples of non-organic foods are precooked/ready-to-cook food and prepared/processed/commercial food. And now, we have two kinds of farming: organic farming[3] (farming with Mother Earth's nutrients only) and non-organic farming (farming with manfactured nutrients).

But what of non-organic farming? Why, suddenly, after many years of men using fertilizer as manure are they eager to move back to organic farming?

These questions are what I will tend to like the crispy lettuce growing in your backyard.

WHY IS NON-ORGANIC FARMING SUDDENLY FACING BACKLASH?

We humans are innovators; we ask questions. You asked questions, probably dozens of them, before picking up this book; perhaps hundreds are in your mind as you are reading. So, it's normal to probe. It is human nature and these questions we ask every day often led to different inventions, like rockets, skyscrapers, and photochromic glasses. But if something new comes into the limelight, why should it be getting backlash all of a sudden? A good question, if you ask me.

One thing that has always come in handy with the invention phase of history is the adverse effect it always has on the natural alternative of the product. For example, think about the invention of industrial machineries. In contrast to their advantages, their fumes also pollute the air and contribute to climate change. Another groundbreaking invention is the introduction of pest control and other farming alternatives (like fertilizers) to natural supplements.

The invention of the (non-organic) industry saved farmers the stress of tilling several hectares of land, but it also affected food crops and soil organisms. Besides these inventions, another factor aided conventional farming[4] and farm products: the grocery store down the road. So, why are these amazing inventions suddenly getting backlash now? Let's dive right in.

- **It has a huge impact on the environment.**

Our environment worsens daily as farmers overuse pesticides and fertilizer; the quality of underground water and other water sources also worsen for the same reason.

The issue with non-organic farming is that the chemicals used can contaminate water supplies by seeping through the soil. NPK—an acronym for Nitrogen (N), Phosphorus (P), and Potassium (K)—is non-toxic in modest doses. But too much of it can negatively affect the natural environment. Plus, nitric oxide is very harmful.

As the work of chemical fertilizer, one method is to perform precisely what it is meant to do, which is to assist plants in growing. But the issue is that it produces what experts call a **dead zone**[5]. When it is present in water, it promotes excess growth of planktons and other aquatic plants. When these plants die, the decomposition process that follows consumes the oxygen that fish and other aquatic creatures need to survive. As a result, waterways near land, which also have the most agricultural runoff, lack fish and other aquatic organisms, which can be interpreted as a negative impact on the local ecology as well as the fishing business.

- **It aids the greenhouse effect.**

Another issue with non-organic farming is that it adds to global warming through the help of Nitrogen. Nitrogen, dubbed the "other greenhouse gas" is just as harmful as carbon dioxide in terms of global warming but less popular. Power plants and automobiles are primary producers of nitrogen in the atmosphere, which exists as nitrous oxide. But applying more nitrogen fertilizer than crops can absorb also plays a significant role.

- **It can contaminate water bodies.**

Irrigation of traditional farming can lead to pesticide runoff, which pollutes rivers and has a negative impact on aquatic ecosystems due to toxic consequences –

consequences like hazardous blue-green algal blooms, which may sometimes harm cattle, wildlife, marine creatures, and us humans. Likewise, chemical buildup in the soil can affect plants and any wildlife or people that eat them.

- **It yields less nutritious food.**

Food crops grown using chemical fertilizers may be less nutritious than they should be. This is because chemical fertilizers aid rapid growth instead of plant health, resulting in products with low nutritional value. As a result, plants will thrive on little more than NPK, but they will be deficient in essential minerals like calcium, zinc, and iron. This may have a little but significant impact on the health of those who consume them.

- **It can cause terminal diseases.**

Chemical fertilizers harm brain development of fetuses and increase the risk of cancer in children and adults. Scientists already know this. The University of Wisconsin c research that found that normal ground-water concentrations of nitrate (a common fertilizer) and pesticides can harm fetuses in development and young children's neurological, endocrine, immunological systems. Sodium nitrate in groundwater was linked to stomach cancer in 1973 and testicular cancer in 1996 in a 1973 research project.

Also, chemical fertilizers may greatly influence the development of methemoglobinemia, also known as blue baby syndrome. This finding was made in a recent study. Researchers believe the illness is caused by feeding infants nitrate-contaminated baby formula made from well water. As a result, the infected infant becomes blue and may go into a coma or die if untreated.

- **It yields food filled with emulsifiers.**

In grocery stores, emulsifiers are used to enhance the texture of food and increase its shelf life. They are present in almost every food, from margarine to ice cream and bread. Emulsifiers, according to most research, can alter gut bacteria and cause Crohn's disease—an inflammation commonly linked to other gut inflammatory disorders.

Since processed food is actually a form of additive, anytime you buy it, you literally inject additives into your body. To extend the shelf life of these processed foods, certain chemicals need to be used. Additionally, processed foods include antibiotics, herbicides, and hormones.

- **It yields food containing Genetically Modified Organisms.**

GMOs (Genetically Modified Organisms) are another risky product that is created by transferring particular characteristics or genes from one creature to another. So, it's better to eat organic foods for health reasons. Also, organic foods don't contain GMOs or industrial pesticides like hexane.

- **It develops resistance traits.**

Nature adapts to fumes, noises, farts, chemicals and nearly everything we throw at it. As a result, non-organic farming pesticides are losing their effectiveness. This means that due to the number of times they have been used for pest control, pests have grown resistant to them. Also, plants have adapted to pesticides throughout the years. This means we need more effective chemicals.

Even though non-organic farming has its use, it also poses certain risks. Using more fertilizer than plants need to grow, whether on a farm or on a lawn, can harm us and the environment. Since chemical fertilizers cause long-lasting damage, it's probably wiser to find other sustainable ways to fertilize the soil.

SHOULD YOU CARE ABOUT ORGANIC FARMING?

I mean, seriously, why should you?

In the 1900s, Albert Howard, F.H. King, Rudolf Steiner, and others who probably started asking questions after their last round of bourbon suggested that animal dung could be used as manure, which would benefit the soil and plants. This belief then led to the groundbreaking idea of organic farming. Unlike non-organic farming that became popular with the invention of mechanized tools, organic farming became popular when farmers started using animal dung to fertilize the soil. This style became the trend until non-organic farming took over, which led to the use of artificial fertilizers and pest control, as I discussed in the previous part of this chapter.

As opposed to non-organic farming, organic farming is a practice that involves growing plants and raising animals naturally. This technique uses organic resources, rather than synthetic chemicals, to maintain soil fertility and the ecological balance, therefore reducing pollution and waste. In other words, organic farming is a farming practice that involves cultivating crops without using synthetic fertilizers or pesticides. Also, the use of genetically engineered organisms isn't allowed.

If you ask me what the difference between organic and non-organic farming is, based on theory and my years of experience, I'll say that non-organic farming relies on chemicals to control pests and weeds and supply plant-worsening nourishment. Synthetic insecticides, herbicides, and fertilizers are included. While on the other hand, organic farming focuses on natural farming practices, like biodiversity and composting to create healthy, abundant food.

Organic production is not just about avoiding conventional chemicals or substituting artificial ingredients for natural ones. In today's world, organic farmers, including you, employ practices that have been used for thousands of years, such as crop rotation and the use of animal manures and green manure to boost soil fertility. This means that in organic production, the interplay between management techniques is key. Biodynamic farmers use different styles to increase and sustain biological diversity and soil fertility.

So, instead of using synthetic input like chemical fertilizers, insecticides, and herbicides, organic farmers rely on natural processes, biodiversity, and cycles that suit local conditions. Most importantly, GMOs are not allowed in organic food. This makes the food more compatible with our body system as it's purely organic.

By now, you're probably confused and, at the same time, looking forward to the benefits of organic farming and organic farm products. Let's get started.

THE FRUITS OF MOVING INTO ORGANIC FARMING

- **It builds healthy soil.**

To grow nutritious food, you must first cultivate good soil. If you treat the soil with toxic pesticides and chemicals, you may end up with soil that cannot flourish on its own. Natural cultivation techniques are significantly superior to chemical soil management. Going on organic farming marks the beginning of everything colorful as laid down by natural laws.

- **It helps fight erosion.**

According to some research, organic fields have 8 inches more topsoil than chemically treated fields and just a third of the erosion loss. As a result, organic farming promotes healthy soil and fights major problems like soil erosion. Erosion has severe consequences that affect land, food supplies, and us.

- **Organic garbage can be reused.**

Organic farming can also help us use our natural resources more efficiently. Natural resources, like plant waste, can be composted and used as soil or fertilizer the following year. Every item we reuse increases our efficiency, since we get to use them again after the first time. As a result, organic gardening can also help reduce waste because most of our trash can be recycled and repurposed. Most importantly, it will save you more money.

- **You don't need to worry about GMOs.**

In organic farming, GMOs are not allowed to be used in organic systems at any level of organic food production, processing, or handling. Because the impact of GMOs on human and environmental health is unknown, organic agriculture takes a cautious approach to farming and promotes natural biodiversity.

- **Organic farming provides safer working conditions.**

Many agricultural laborers die each year as a result of using pesticide, particularly in third-world nations. Even in areas where farmers practice modern farming and understand the need for safety, the risk of cancer is still higher in farmers than in the general public, owing to pesticide usage. The safer working conditions for farmers and farm laborers are one of the best parts of not using pesticides.

- **It improves exceptional biodiversity.**

Pesticides are harmful to plants, insects, and higher life forms. They endanger the survival of some weed species and also reduce overall biodiversity in fields and adjacent areas. Bird food, for example, has seriously reduced because of this. Many studies show that the number of bird species rises on ecologically managed farms. Crop rotations employed in ecological agriculture increase biodiversity while also protecting farmers from economic disasters caused by damaged crops or declining prices.

- **You don't have to be concerned about water and food contamination.**

When no pesticides are used, there is also less risk of food contamination. Additionally, several studies have found that animals and people that consume organic food are more fertile. On the other hand, organic food can be contaminated by persistent, airborne pesticides in the field and therefore not be considered pesticide-free. And now that pesticides in drinking water are becoming a growing concern worldwide, diving into organic farming within your home is just be the best step to take.

Moving into organic farming celebrates the rule of nature. It brings you and I closer to natural ways of farming. It also has many health benefits for everyone. Now, if you are wondering why you should move into organic farming, here are the reasons.

GENUINE REASONS YOU SHOULDN'T TURN YOUR BACK ON ORGANIC FARMING

- **Organic farming yields more nutrients.**

Previously, some researchers gathered and analyzed vegetables, fruits, and cereals from both organic and conventional farms. Unlike food from conventional farms, food from organic farms is higher in nutrients such as vitamins, enzymes, minerals, and other micronutrients. This is because organic farms are managed and nourished using eco-friendly methods.

- **It conserves agricultural diversities.**

We hear a lot about extinct species these days, and we should be worried. About 75 percent of the agricultural diversity of crops was wiped off in the last hundred years. Leaning toward one type of farming is a formula for future disaster. Potatoes are a classic example. Back then, there were several kinds available in the market. Today, just one potato species reigns supreme. This is bad because if pests wipe out the last potato species available today, we will no longer have potatoes. This is why, to ensure a sustainable future, we need organic agricultural practices that will yield disease- and pest-resistant crops.

- **You are investing in natural farming.**

Buying food from organic farms is a pretty good bet for a more cost-effective future. Recently, most governments have provided substantial subsidies and tax breaks to conventional agricultural practices. This has led to the expansion of commercially manufactured foods, which has raised the risk of severe diseases such as cancer. It is high time governments invested in organic agricultural technology to solve these issues and protect the future. It all starts with you buying food from well-known organic sources.

- **Your food is sure to taste better and more natural.**

If you've ever tried organically grown foods, you would know that they have a more natural flavor. The rich soil they grow in is responsible for their natural and wonderful flavor. Organic producers usually prioritize quality over quantity.

- **Again, you don't have to worry about GMOs.**

Statistics show that genetically modified organisms (GMOs) are infecting natural food supplies alarmingly, with far-reaching consequences. Plus, the fact that they can't be identified makes them even more dangerous. As a result, the only way to reduce the harmful effects of GMOs is to eat organic foods bought from reliable sources.

- **It helps boost the nutritional value of the food you eat.**

Organic crops are produced on soil that is healthy and biologically active. While organic farms have lower yields and produce crops that take longer to mature than crops grown on non-organic farms, their crops are rich in essential antioxidants, minerals, and vitamins.

- **It decreases the intake of unused antibiotics.**

Most non-organic livestock producers mix growth hormones, medicines, and feed supplements with high-grain diets to force their animals to grow faster and larger. As a result, these animals produce more milk and eggs each day. In reality, animals on conventional farms are usually overworked to the point that they suffer from major reproductive and/or other health issues that call for the use of antibiotics. In contrast to this, almost all synthetic animal drugs are prohibited under the National Organic Program (NOP) guideline. In the end, healthier animals provide healthier meat, milk, dairy products, and eggs.

Organic food production practices enhance biodiversity, the nutrient cycle, and both plant and animal health. Organic farmers are not allowed to use toxic synthetic pesticides, artificial fertilizers, unnecessary hormones, or antibiotics. Instead, they must employ techniques that repair, maintain, and improve soil and ecosystem health. GMOs, artificial additives, and trans fats are also not allowed.

There are vast differences between organic and non-organic farming, especially when it comes to the advancement of technology for non-organic farming. However, technological advancement doesn't always mean it makes our food and health better.

- **It soothes your soul.**

Nothing fills your spirit with joy like a day spent having fun in the dirt. When you're away from screens, work, and traffic, and tending to the plants in your garden, you can feel the tension melt away. Imagine proudly admiring a baby veggie that popped out of nowhere and anticipating the day when it will be ripe and ready to pick, or shouting with delight as you call out to your children and partner, or watching your young ones help themselves to lunch in the garden, as they sneak a little something off a vine or two, perhaps a day or several too early. Those are the moments that stand out and soothe your soul. Simple pleasures like these make life worth living. Gardening in the fresh air is not only satisfying, but also beneficial to you. To reduce your tension, get some fresh air and vitamin D, then have your fill of some delicious cuisine.

ORGANIC VS. NON-ORGANIC FARMING: WHICH ONE WINS?

In conventional farming, the farmer treats or fumigates his farm with harsh chemicals before planting to get rid of any natural fungicides present. Petrol-based fertilizers are also used to improve the soil. Organic farmers prepare and enrich their soil before planting by using natural fertilizers such as manure, bone meal, and mussel fertilizer.

The non-organic farmer would soak the seeds in fungicides and insecticides before sowing them to keep insects and pests at bay. Chemicals are also added to the irrigation water to keep insects from damaging the seeds. On the other hand, the organic farmer doesn't soak his seeds in any chemical solution or irrigate newly planted seeds with chemical-laced water. In fact, he refuses to irrigate with municipal water, which is chlorinated to kill germs. Instead, during the dry months, he relies on rain or harvests rainwater.

To remove weeds once the seeds germinate, the conventional farmer applies weedicide. But the organic farmer doesn't use such methods. Instead, his plan is to manually weed the farm, which is stressful. Then, if the organic farmer prefers, he may burn the weeds or allow animals to eat them.

Who do you think is doing it better? And more importantly, who would you buy your produce from?

KEY TAKEAWAYS

- Organic farming is characterized by the use of natural ways of farming.
- Non-organic farming, however, uses mechanized ways of farming.
- Organic farming benefits our health significantly.
- The use of synthetic input to grow non-organic farm products is unhealthy.

---

1. A chemical or natural substance added to soil or land to increase its fertility.
2. Non-organic farming is the classification of artificial based farming.
3. Hello, new word - organic farming is fully using earth substances. CHECK FOR MORE IN THE CHAPTER.
4. Non-organic farming
5. In the words of experts concerned, Dead Zones are hypoxic areas in the world's oceans and large lakes. Hypoxia occurs when dissolved oxygen concentration falls to or below 2ml of O_2/liter.

2

WHAT YOU NEED TO BE PREPARED

By now, different ideas of things you can plant are probably racing through your mind—like carrot, cabbage, lettuce, or maybe mustard. Yes, it's really a good idea to go organic. In fact, I strongly suggest you get a green T-shirt with the tagline 'GO ORGANIC'!

It's okay. It's all fun. But you should also know that organic farming is systematic farming, so you need to have detailed knowledge of your surroundings. What I'm trying to say is that going organic is all about knowing what to do, when to do it, and how to do it. So, before you go green, you must first learn to till.

The transition of man from a nomadic hunter to a sedentary farmer might have happened by accident, yet man's knowledge taught him a lot about his environment, like why he can rear dogs and rabbits but not cougars and honey badgers. Man's knowledge of his environment helped him pick the best spot for his organic agriculture, including choosing loamy soil over a hard clay soil[1].

So, in this chapter, I will discuss what you need to prepare for organic farming. But don't panic! Everything you need or will need is within your reach—well, except a few other things. Now, count that as one of the advantages of organic farming. So, as you know, organic farming uses organic materials in manure, land, pest control, and plant growth, unlike non-organic farming. And this can sometimes be selective, but as your farm guide, I will share everything you need to know to become a good farmer. Just stick around.

GETTING STARTED WITH YOUR VEGETABLE GARDENING

Now that you have decided to go green, the points below are different tips you can apply when you are about to start your vegetable garden.

1. Choose a good location.

Before you dig a hole or plant a seed, sit down, and think about what you want your vegetable garden to achieve. You must first check if you have the room and necessary conditions to grow what you want to produce in the first place. The known storyline is the most familiar one.

Choose a place with sunlight: It's no secret that veggies need full sunlight, which means they need at least 6 hours of sunlight every day. Most plants, on the other hand, thrive with more water. So that site will do for your garden if it receives full sunlight for 6-10 hours daily, but that's not a guarantee. As an alternative, if your land does not get enough sunlight, try removing trees, but only if you can do it without side effects. So, before you start, think carefully. If clearing trees is not possible, choose another spot that gets enough sunlight.

Don't forget the essence of water: Water is essential for our lives and that of plants too. Our lives would not be complete without it; trust me, nothing can replace H_2O^2. This is something you should remember while choosing a site for your vegetable garden. Vegetable gardens should be located near a water source. If you have to pull a water hose 20 feet simply to water the garden, you would probably get fed up with the task and abandon it. So, place your garden near a water source to make it as easy as possible to maintain. But if doing this makes your garden not meet your other criteria, try installing a water hose to make watering easier for you. You should also consider placing your garden near the pump if your house has a well.

Level up your ground: Your garden's base is the soil. You can always improve your soil, but if you have a spot in your yard that already has good soil, that would be the best place to start. If you wish to improve the soil later, you'll have a much better foundation to work with. It will boost your garden and give it yet another reason to grow. If you're not sure your soil is healthy, do a soil test. Saturate the area with water and leave it for a day. Grab a handful of soil the next day and squeeze it as hard as you can. If the dirt breaks up as soon as you open your palm, then you know it's too sandy.

Give it air: Before you start your vegetable garden, make sure your choice location allows for enough air—don't make it stuffy! Don't place the plants too close to one another or you'll limit the flow of air. Instead, find a site for your vegetable garden that will offer plenty of room to breathe. This means that you must be able to feel the wind when it's blowing in your garden. Mold and mildew can grow on your plants if your garden isn't ventilated enough to keep them healthy. These diseases spread easily and can destroy your garden. Airflow is one of the most important ways to prevent these diseases.

Avoid frost pockets: Frost pockets[3] can turn a gardener's life upside down. Due to the difference in their densities, cold air sinks and warm air rises. As a result, cold air could find its way to the lowest area of your garden, where it could settle and cause frost pockets. Try to stay away from frost pockets because a seedling can quickly die if it is planted in one. Keep an eye out for possible frost pockets. Remove them from your garden if you get the chance to. To avoid planting in specific areas, you'll need to mark out these areas on your garden plan.

2. Know your budget.

Before you start your vegetable garden, you should have an idea of what your budget is. This will help you tailor what your garden should really look like and also help you know if you are financially ready to go organic. But if you don't know how to plan a budget for your garden, these few tips will help you. Trust me—they've helped gardeners before us.

Gardeners know that gardening is a satisfying hobby, but it's also time-consuming and costly. Building a garden is expensive, as are seedlings and fertilizer. Not to mention the extra water you use during dry weather conditions. So, why should you bother growing your own vegetables when you can get a weekly organic produce box from your local food co-op? The answer is that it all depends on how you go about your gardening endeavors.

Get to seed swap: Shopping for seeds can be a lot of fun, so you don't have to worry if it will be boring; also, if you're careful, you may find some great deals on the products. Even more interesting and cheaper is a **seed swap**. A seed swap, just as the name implies, is where everyone brings seeds from the previous year and trades them with one another. Saving seeds in fall is also essential. If they're not Monsanto-patented, saving seeds is free.

Search your garden for natural supplies: Sometimes, nature provides free items that might help you get the most bang for your buck when gardening. For example, from tomato stakes to gorgeous oriental fences and arbors, bamboo poles sold in garden centers range from $1 apiece to $10 each or higher, depending on their size and shape. Meanwhile, other garden centers have a yard full of bamboo that they would gladly let you take them off their hands if they could. This is just one example. If you find yourself thinking, "Oh, I wish I had the money to buy something for the garden," try to find of a free, local alternative.

Cutting can be an alternative: You probably think storing seeds is excellent for vegetables, but who grows blueberries or dogwood trees from seed? That is correct, nobody does. Many vegetables are hard to grow from seed; most don't grow "true" from seed since they breed asexually (meaning they are genetic clones). The good news is that cuttings may be used to breed most perennials, shrubs, vines, and trees. Find a neighbor or a friend who has the plant you want, remove a few pencil-sized sticks from it, pot them up in moist perlite, and you should see roots and leaves emerge within a few weeks or months.

Try recycling and upcycling: As you already know, plants are pretty expensive. Planters, pavers, arbors, and other hardscape materials can make your budget shoot up quickly. Isn't it true, though, that one man's trash pile is another man's goldmine? Almost anything can be turned into a planter, from the old bathtub in your backyard to a wooden pallet. A satellite dish set on a pole has been used to create arbors, while bedsprings have been used to create climbing trellises. When you go overboard, upcycling might make you feel like you have a yard full of rubbish. So, use restraint when upcycling.

Go totally organic: Choosing natural approaches is great for saving money. Insecticides are costly, but introducing beneficial insects to your garden (good bugs that eat the bad bugs) is simple and completely free. Herbicides are the same. It's possible to remove weeds by hand; you could smother them with black plastic or layers of cardboard and wood chips, or even get some goats to eat them up (they love eating plants like kudzu, poison ivy, and thorny briars).

Work on your own soil components: Organic fertilizers, such as bat guano and feather meal, can be expensive. So, when you consider what they contain—animal by-products (such as bat guano) and organic matter (such as shredded bark and cocoa husks)—buying them seems like a waste of money. If you don't have any poultry or other livestock to get manure from, you could always find a friend or local farmer who would let you clear out their barn. So instead, make a thick black compost[4] by mixing the manure with wood shavings or grass clippings or leaves—whatever organic matter you can get your hands on. Composting isn't the only way to make your soil richer; you could also use living plants, also known as cover crops. Also, if you live near a beach, you could gather seaweed for a boost of micronutrients. Just be sure to rinse it thoroughly in fresh water after harvesting it to remove salt from it before using it.

Benefit from free compost and mulch: It is rare for tree-cutting enterprises to have large amounts of mulch on hand that they are willing to give away for free. However, several towns often turn green garbage into compost and mulch, giving it away for free or at a small price. However, use these freebies at your own risk, as they may include garbage or seeds of invasive plants.

3. Is your soil good and ready?

Soil that is rich in nutrients is essential for effective gardening. Plenty of underground animal and plant activity, such as earthworms and fungi, is a sign of good soil. Soil rich in organic matter is dark and crumbles from the roots of plants when you pull them from it. A healthy, well-distributed root system is another sign of good soil. These few tips will help you know if your soil is suitable for planting. You don't need to contact a soil specialist.

The soil color: In a healthy garden, the soil should have a beautiful, dark, black hue. Unhealthy soil looks more like dirt: brown and dry. When wet, this poor soil will turn into brown muck. Healthy soil absorbs rainwater well and doesn't have a muddy appearance. Most plants have green foliage, with a bright green hue. Plants with many hues, such as kale and red lettuce, also have a bright color. If the leaves are yellow, it is most likely due to a nitrogen shortage. Remember that the nutrients in our soil are the same ones that grow into the plants we eat.

Take a cutting of a sickly plant and place it in a cup of water. A bacterial issue in the soil may be the cause of murky water. The plant may have a virus if the water is clear. Leaves with fuzz or hairs developing on them might be infected with fungus. The soil may contain too much nitrogen, or the climate in your area may be too hot for this plant to grow if it isn't bearing fruit. The plant should either be completely destroyed in these situations, or only the diseased leaves should be removed, depending on how serious the case is. In the end, it all comes down to how much of your plant was affected.

Check if bugs are attacking the plants: The fact that bugs are attacking your garden plants is probably a sign that your plants are weak and may not be growing in healthy soil. On the other hand, strong, vigorous plants have the ability to fight pests naturally. Isn't it amazing? Adding wood chips or shredded leaves on top of the soil to keep the temperature down is a good idea if there is a problem with the soil's temperature.

Check your roots: By the way, this does not mean your genealogy or family tree[5]. I mean your plants' roots. So, while identifying good soil from the roots of your plants, do not rush through the process of checking the roots, as it may be very useful. Be as gentle as possible. Digging up the roots of a tiny annual plant is a great place to start. If you don't mind losing the plant, pluck it and carefully study its roots. Consider replacing your plant with some of the qualities listed above if the roots seem healthy to you. The roots should be long, well-spread, and free. They should not be mushy or soggy. If this is the case, then drainage might be the problem. You could solve this problem over time by adding more organic material to the surface of your soil, such as compost, shredded leaves, grass clippings, plant trimmings, and so on. You could try adding some peat moss to your soil for a quick fix. Roots highly depend on soil conditions. When soil quality is low, roots won't develop or spread freely. Here's another example of soil that may benefit from being covered with compost. This will provide nutrients to the soil and make it more suitable for root growth.

Compaction: Compaction occurs when hard soil stops water from reaching plant roots. Compacted soil makes it hard for roots to develop and earthworms to burrow. A thin wire can be used to test the soil for compaction, though highly compacted dirt might trap it or bend it at the top. The wire should be able to slip at least a foot into the soil without bending and with ease. Compaction is a common problem in gardens with clay soil due to the soil's density. Clay can be used to create successful gardens, although it may be harder. For plants to use these nutrients, the soil pH has to be monitored from time to time in clay soils as opposed to sandy soils.

Know your soil workability: Worried about workability? It is the ease with which dirt can be worked on. Even though our gardening approach discourages tilling and excessive digging in the garden, you must assess the soil's workability before you start planting. You know your soil is unworkable if it's hard to pull tools through it or if pulling tools through it makes the soil form big, lumpy clods. Another sign that the soil is unworkable is that you can't easily dig holes for planting with your hands. To prepare a garden bed for planting, you don't have to put much work into it! Although most gardeners might think they would need to till the garden bed in this situation, you should only till a garden bed in the first year if you absolutely have to, but I would never recommend it. For example, you would be tilling in compost, peat moss, or worm castings, all of which are excellent soil supplements. This is because tilling kills soil organisms; it also creates a layer that water can't penetrate and leaves less crop waste behind. A garden's workability/compaction can be improved over time by covering the soil with compost.

Check for soil organisms: Another way to know if your soil is ready to house a garden is to check for soil organisms. But how can you do this? It's simple. Grab a shovel and dig about six inches deep. Observe the dirt. If you look closely at the soil's surface, you should see plenty of life—spiders, ants, earthworms, etc. You should be able to spot no less than **ten living organisms**. The soil might be unhealthy if you count less than ten living organisms. You must always keep soil organisms in mind because they are beneficial. Pests that damage plants are a negative thing.

When it comes to inspecting soil quality, this is perhaps the most obvious test you can do. Less disease and pest problems are likely to occur if there are more insects in the soil. For the plants, these microorganisms each play their role in breaking down organic materials.

Check for earthworms: Again, dig about six inches deep and count only the earthworms that you find there. The more earthworms you find, the better. At the very least, you should find three earthworms. In the garden, there should be many earthworms. Aerating[6] the soil by drilling it, earthworms are natural tillers. They help the soil breathe. They feed on organic materials, and their castings replenish the soil with beneficial bacteria, enzymes, plant nutrients, and organic matter. Because earthworms feed on organic matter, a lack of earthworms in the soil indicates a lack of organic matter. Earthworms can be bought to replenish the soil's health and supply nutrients to the soil's surface. Though buying worms is a quick fix, you'd be surprised at how quickly the worms will "emerge" from your soil if you start adding things like compost and coffee grounds. Wigglers love this type of food!

Water infiltration: A cylinder-shaped container is ideal for this. Remove the cylinder's bottom. A coffee can is an excellent example of what you could use. Push the container vertically into the earth until only a few inches remain above the soil surface. Add water to the container and let it sit for a while. Placing a mark at the water's height is a good idea. Keep track of how long it takes the water to be entirely absorbed into the soil by setting a timer. Do this several times until absorption slows down and your timings become similar. If these more regular timings are slower than a half-inch to an inch per hour, then you may have compacted dirt on your hands.

Knowing these points will help you know if your soil is good and ready for gardening. But if you find out that your soil is not too good for the garden to work, you can fix it.

Before starting, you should note that fixing soil can be a lengthy process, but don't give up just yet! Be patient with your garden and have fun with it! If you haven't started making your own compost (which I strongly suggest you do), you could buy bags of compost at a shop or check with your local landscaping businesses. You should be able to find compost near your yard. If you're lucky, some cities even provide free compost! Each fall, gardeners who cover their soil with 1–2 inches of compost have no difficulty with poor soil. Mulch the entire garden if necessary to battle weeds and control soil temperature. Taking these steps should solve most soil problems.

4. Do you have your gardening tools ready?

If you're thinking of starting a garden, you surely know you'll need more than a handful of tools to get the job done. However, you don't need a shed full of equipment for every plant you want to grow. So, save yourself (and your pocketbook of the garden tools) a trip to the garden center by sticking to these tools I have provided for you.

Trowel: A handheld trowel is essential for many common gardening activities, such as breaking up clumps of dirt, digging small holes, transplanting seedlings, and even digging out weeds. Both container and large-scale gardeners use a trowel regularly. If you can only afford one piece of entry-level gardening equipment, make it this one. Choose one with a strong metal blade and firm wooden handle.

A hose/watering can: If you're planting directly in the ground, get a hose that's long enough to stretch from your tap to your garden. Consider adding a sprayer attachment that will allow you to adjust the flow and pressure of the water. If you're only doing container gardening, a watering can might suffice—look for one that's lightweight and easy to be handled, even when full. Use water early in the morning when the temperature is low for the best result. Avoid watering in the afternoon because water evaporates too fast during the day; avoid watering at night, too, or the soil will become soggy and serve as a breeding ground for deadly fungi and bacteria.

Garden rake: Garden rakes generally have a long wooden handle with metal-tipped tines to pick up grass clippings and other loose particles. In addition to weeding, they help you level the soil. When planting on uneven or rough terrain, try switching to a garden hoe with greater weight; this might help you chop and clear unruly areas and weeds with ease.

Pruning shears: A robust pair of pruning shears can come in handy whether you're gathering fresh food or trimming your berry bushes. First, snip the plant's node (where the branches meet the stem in a Y shape) for a clean cut. Then, invest in a set of loppers for branches 2 inches thick or thicker after your garden matures.

Angled shovel: A shovel looks simple enough, but you might be amazed at how many variations are available in the shop. First, choose an angled shovel (a shovel with a triangular head) to help you dig holes, shift dirt, and reposition plants. If you're starting a large landscaping bed, a square garden spade can help you make cleaner cuts, but an angled shovel will be enough for most beginners.

Other tools include:

- Gardening gloves
- Kneeling pad
- Handheld weeder
- Sprinkler
- Wheelbarrow

KEY TAKEAWAYS

- Knowing whether your soil is good and ready for your vegetable gardening is very important.
- Get your tools ready.

---

1. I am not saying hard clay cannot house any plants. Loamy soil is just better suited to most plant varieties.
2. Chemical formula for water
3. A frost pocket, also known as a frost hollow, is an area of land which has a higher risk and longer season of frost.
4. Decayed organic material used as a fertilizer for growing plants.
5. Even family history is incorporated as a tree!
6. Aeration involves perforating the soil with small holes to allow air, water, and nutrients to penetrate the grass roots.

3

BEST METHODS FOR OPTIMAL SUCCESS

Now that you have started thinking of different spots in your home to use as your vegetable garden, you should also note the different methods you can try to grow your vegetables. You don't need to freak out just because I said there were multiple ways of doing this. Just know that these methods are here to help you grow the best veggies; also, different lands have different methods that work best for them. You wouldn't want to offend Mother Earth by using the wrong method, would you? I know you would love to have a good veggie pluck that speaks well to your soul. But to get all these things, you must first learn the different methods you can adopt for optimal success in your gardening. Do you want to know them now? *Read on.*

There are different methods that can help you develop your vegetable garden; perhaps, I should call them planting systems. These systems consist of various features that will help you go organic, and the best ones that will surely help you succeed are:

- Traditional vegetable garden
- Permaculture
- No-dig
- Raised beds
- Square foot gardening

However, before you start testing which method will work best for your garden, I have some really important factors I would like you to keep in mind. It is no big deal; actually, it's all geared toward giving you the best results. But remember, if you want to get it right, you must do it exactly.

FACTORS TO CONSIDER BEFORE CHOOSING YOUR GARDENING METHOD

- **Never underrate the size of your site.**

Even though this might sound quite repetitive, note that I wouldn't keep repeating it if it weren't so important. The size of your site is crucial to your plants' success. But know that you may grow vegetables conventionally if you have a large yard and wish to maximize your yield. On the other hand, these low-maintenance gardening strategies are ideal if you have a small or medium-sized yard. Vegetables can grow successfully in a small informal area if flower borders are planted between the beds.

- **The compatibility of your soil for growing conditions.**

When you move to a new house, you may not give much thought to the soil's health, but you should if you want to grow fruits and vegetables. Heavy clay may be just as hard to deal with as thin, rocky soil, and poor drainage will always make your crops not grow. Improved soil conditions can be achieved through traditional methods such as deep digging and adding significant amounts of organic matter, like compost or leaf mold. Other options (such as using elevated beds) are described in the sections that follow. In every garden, the soil is critical, but even more so in a vegetable garden. Your vegetable garden's soil must be rich in organic materials.

- **The crops you want to grow.**

Before choosing your gardening method, you should also consider the crops you want to grow. This will largely be determined by your taste in food. Still, you should also consider the available space. Herbs, a few high-value crops, and a variety of salad vegetables can be grown in a small garden, for example.

- **The quantities and spacing.**

This may not have crossed your mind earlier, but it's okay. That's why I'm telling you now before I talk about the different methods for growing a successful vegetable garden. Producing enough food for your household is vital, but you must also pay attention to the planting directions on seed packs to ensure that you provide enough space between plants for them to grow well. You should never grow the same veggies year after year, no matter what gardening method you use. Crop rotation is a term used to describe this practice.

Now that you know the four important things that you must bear in mind before choosing your gardening method, let's get started on the methods.

FIVE METHODS FOR GROWING YOURGARDEN

It takes time and effort to plan the ideal vegetable garden layout. Think of all the things you have to consider! To thrive, your veggies will need a lot of sunlight, water, nutrients, and tender loving care. It's important to plan your vegetable garden's layout before you begin planting. Vegetables can be grown vertically, hydroponically, or in containers, if you have a small yard (or none at all). However, just as I said before, there are four gardening methods that can help you achieve a successful garden.

The Traditional Vegetable Garden

The typical vegetable garden is the kitchen garden of a rural house, where rows upon rows of beautiful vegetables are laid out in a grid pattern. Those with little free time or those who only wish to have a small vegetable patch might find this discouraging. Fortunately for modern gardeners, times have changed. Now you can make the most of your area while still giving your plants what they need, thanks to several planting strategies.

Vegetable gardens in rows and blocks are ideal for those lucky enough to have a spacious backyard.

However, some crops, like pumpkins, thrive better in pots, while others, like maize, do better in rows. Therefore, I've included this information for each vegetable garden design. Of course, there are pros and cons to each design, but some designs are better for pest management than others.

The first garden design is:

Narrow Rows

Also known as the market gardening technique. When it comes to growing many veggies at once, this vegetable garden design is the most effective option. Rows are less than 2 feet wide, making it simple to manage crop rotation and take care of the plants. Everything, save creepers and grains, should be consumed, including all veggies (and corn). It's the best design for crops that require a lot of effort or plants that grow continuously, like beans and tomatoes.

Benefits of Narrow Row Garden Design

- Easy access to crop cultivation and harvesting facilities.
- Rows can be tilled in a single pass.
- Drip irrigation is an efficient irrigation system.
- Low-cost implementation and maintenance.
- Everything about it exudes beauty.

- Accessibility is excellent.

Disadvantages of Narrow Row Garden Design

- If many rows of the same crop are planted together, the risk of pests and diseases will increase.
- Individual rows are too small for wheelbarrow access (although the main access path is wide enough for this).
- Access gap between rows is a huge waste of space.

The second garden design is:

Wide Rows and Blocks

Wide rows and blocks is another approach contrary to the narrow rows, and it's quite common among home gardeners looking to make the most of small plots. More crops can be grown in the same area by using a wider row spacing of 4 feet; however, getting to the middle of the row is harder. A good arrangement for intense cropping or continuous-harvest plants, such as beans and tomatoes, is free of vines and crawlers.

Benefits of Wide Rows and Blocks Garden Design

- For smaller plots, it is a more cost-effective

design.

- Row spacing might be broader to accommodate wheelbarrows.
- Drip irrigation is an efficient irrigation system.
- Low-cost implementation and maintenance
- Everything about it exudes beauty.

Disadvantages of Wide Rows and Blocks Garden Design

- Reduced airflow around crops leads to more pests and diseases.
- The middle of the row is the most difficult to maintain and harvest.
- In most farming systems, crops are all sown and harvested at the same time.

Permaculture

The second-best method for growing your garden successfully is called permaculture. Permaculture combines land, resources, people, and the environment through mutually beneficial synergies, replicating the waste-free, closed-loop processes seen in a wide range of natural systems. Permaculture researches and implements comprehensive solutions that may be used in rural and urban settings of any size.

In permaculture gardening, you plan your garden to fit in with your surroundings. While still serving human requirements, a permaculture garden design also considers ecology and climate. Permaculture gardening also improves soil quality by adding nutrients so that you are always renewing the earth while improving the health of your plants. Permaculture principles boil down to three things: caring for the Earth, caring for others, and taking only what is fair (and returning any extras).

Anyone who wants to raise their own food in a sustainable way should try permaculture gardening. A vegetable garden built on permaculture principles will use natural processes to boost growth and yield many fruits and vegetables.

Before you start a permaculture garden, here are some important things to note:

Know your surroundings very well: Since permaculture is about planning to fit in with your surroundings, before you start permaculture, you must learn about the natural plants, insects, and predators that live in and around your planting area. Keep an eye out for the areas of the garden that get the most sunlight. Look for any terrain slopes that can store rainwater. Can your garden's special qualities give you an edge? For example, towering native plants in your permaculture system might serve as a living trellis for new plants.

Choose plants that can work with your environment: When choosing what to plant, study your environment to find out which annual and perennial plants flourish there. Then, choose crops that attract beneficial insects, prevent pests, and organically enrich your soil for companion planting. Plant butterfly-attracting flowers, insect-repelling herbs, and green manure crops that fix nitrogen in your soil over time to gradually boost your soil's nutritional levels.

Design the garden layout: Use your knowledge of your surroundings and the plants you wish to grow to create your garden. Consider your light needs, water sources, and environment when deciding where to plant your desired crops in the garden. Then, maximize your space by stacking plants. Plant herbaceous ground cover, shrubs in the middle, and trees on top for best results.

Create your garden beds: The principles of permaculture urge gardeners to use the least amount of energy and cause the least possible damage when breaking ground and making new beds. In the backyard, spot planting and sheet mulching are often done with sodding. When you do spot planting, you dig a hole and plant in a tiny area that was formerly grass. Fill the hole with compost or slow-release organic fertilizer.

Spreading straw mulch or wood chip mulch around the perimeter can keep your soil moist and keep out weeds. Adding bare root trees or boosting the number and diversity of perennial flowers in a meadow region can benefit from spot planting.

Begin planting: First, develop your large plants to provide shade for any smaller plants that are more vulnerable to direct sunlight. Then, check your plan one last time to ensure that plants with similar water and light needs are not randomly thrown together.

Mulch the topsoil with organic material: Permaculture gardening principles do not support the use of chemical weed killers; so, apply an organic mulch layer after planting to control weeds and keep your soil moist. Leaves, newspapers, straws, wood chips, shredded bark, and grass clippings are common mulch materials.

Use manure to fertilize soil: Instead of using artificial fertilizers[1], use natural compost that is rich in organic materials. Manure and kitchen wastes, which may be stored in a compost container, are common composting options. Worm castings and worm tea are also excellent choices since they are loaded with nutrients and boost the number of beneficial microorganisms in your soil.

Use a watering system that is both effective and eco-friendly: Use only as much water as your garden needs to grow. A low-waste drip irrigation system is another great option for watering your soil directly and reducing evaporation. Collect rainwater from your roof gutters so you can reuse it in your irrigation system.

Instead of fighting nature, a permaculture garden makes use of natural elements, like sunlight, wind, and water.

Benefits of Permaculture

There are many benefits you can gain from using permaculture:

Waste reduction: Permaculture can help reduce a lot of waste. The goal of permaculture is to make the most effective use of our resources. This also means that nothing should be wasted and that our resources should serve the public or the environment. As a result, if people use this method, our waste output will be much less than it is with conventional agriculture. This will positively impact the environment since far less trash would need to be burnt or tossed in landfills.

It leads to less air pollution: The goal of permaculture is to make agricultural operations more sustainable and protect our environment, so it strives to reduce our carbon footprint. Because of permaculture, less agricultural machinery is needed, which reduces the amount of air pollution. Also, compared to traditional agriculture, the distance covered by permaculture is much shorter. As a result, air quality will improve and global warming will reduce as fewer greenhouse gases get released into our environment.

It uses renewable energy: Permaculture also encourages gardeners to use renewable energy in their garden. Instead of using non-renewable fossil fuels, we should use renewable energy sources in every aspect of our everyday lives. Besides electricity, we can use renewable energy sources like biodiesel or other chemicals that can speed up our leap from fossil fuels to renewable ones.

You have ethical benefits: Permaculture has many practical advantages, but it also has some ethical advantages. Permaculture strives to improve the quality of life for all living things, not just people. So, avoid factory farming and any other method that involves raising animals in unusual places. Also, permaculture should be favored over conventional agricultural practices, as it is a more ethical, eco-friendly and animal-friendly approach to farming.

It adopts organic farming: As an extra benefit, permaculture also strives for maximum organicity in agricultural operations. Permaculture focuses on using natural fertilizers over artificial ones, which helps make the final product as organic as possible. What's more, permaculture urges the use of organic animal feed, rather than concentrated feed, as is the case in traditional agriculture. Permaculture, unlike traditional agriculture, aims to make farming as natural as possible.

Is Permaculture Cost-Effective?

Growing plants traditionally is more expensive than using permaculture methods. Pesticides and fertilizers, for example, are not necessary expenses. The less need for maintenance in permaculture systems means less money spent on labor. Most of the time, watering and mulching are all that's needed.

No-dig Gardening

It's easy to see why folks came up with the no-dig gardening technique! Digging takes time, distributes weed seeds, and may dry up light soils quickly. The no-dig approach, on the other hand, may not be appropriate for severely compacted soils. Creating narrow beds between 15-cm-high planks and fixing them in the ground with hammered pegs will increase your chances of success. A mulch of straw, sawdust, and grass clippings is placed on top of the newspaper layers, and then soil is covered with these materials. This must be watered thoroughly before adding a layer of compost and about 6cm of soil, which is the layer your seeds will be planted in.

Growing with the no-dig method is tempting. You get rich soil; plus, it's a great way to get rid of weed infestation in your garden. Of course, digging will affect the soil's health, but then you won't be doing any harm by avoiding it. Fungi and worms are examples of beneficial microorganisms that help plants nourish their roots. However, you need plenty of biological matter. Compost materials include leaves, well-rotted manure, and green trash. You could also buy compost in bags that are peat-free.

Benefits of No-dig Gardening

No-dig gardening has many benefits:

It protects soil food: Healthy, productive garden soils sustain a varied soil food web and the complicated symbiosis between microorganisms and plant roots. Hairs of mycorrhizal mycelium fungus, which are a hundred times finer than root hairs, serve as vital pathways for moving soil nutrients and carbohydrates to plant roots. Tilling and digging the soil disrupts and destroys this complex web of life. This soil organism can survive on unaltered soil. On the other hand, no-dig gardens have a better-balanced population of soil biota, indicating a more natural balance between soil pests and predators.

Weed reduction: When soil is dug, weed seeds that have been dormant for a long time become active. Since they get direct sunlight, they'll grow and flourish. Those seeds, however, would remain dormant forever if left undisturbed under the soil's surface. Although using the no-dig approach doesn't rule out the chances of getting weeds. After all, birds and even the wind might carry some weed seeds to your garden. Still, no-dig gardening makes weeding unnecessary by using mulch instead.

It saves water: In no-dig gardening (mulching), compost and other organic elements are applied to the soil's surface in layers. Soil is shaded by these layers, yet water freely passes through. So, mulching keeps the soil moist and reduces evaporation, both of which are important for healthy root growth. Unfortunately, gardeners and farmers all around the globe are under a lot of stress due to water limitations. Because of this, we must all use strategies that will help our gardens flourish when there isn't enough water.

It saves time and energy: Whether you dig your soil by hand or with a power tool, not digging saves you time and energy. Even though applying mulch to the garden regularly takes time, the no-dig approach is far less stressful.

Raised Beds

Raised beds use the same principles as no-dig gardening. Still, they're more substantial since they're made of big, earthen containers filled with organic matter. They can be made from durable materials, like bricks, railway sleepers, and wood crates or boards. Compost is used to fill raised beds higher than the surrounding ground, keeping the soil drier. This design prevents soil and drainage problems. Although walkways connecting beds take up more space in your garden, they make it easier to reach your plants and keep soil from being compacted when people walk on them. Also, the deeper the soil, the more it will make up for the lowered ceiling height.

Raised beds typically have a frame, but you have complete control over what frame material to use. Raised bed frames are usually made from wood or strong plastic. But they can also be made from other materials, such as stones, cinder blocks, bricks, paver patios, concrete fragments (from the recent sidewalk restoration), corrugated metal, straw bales, and so on. This means you could use new or salvaged materials to make them unique to your home and landscape. Of course, it's unnecessary to create a raised bed from scratch if you don't want to; raised beds are also available as kits.

Benefits of Raised Bed Gardening

- There are fewer weeds.
- Better water retention in regions with super-sandy soil.
- Better drainage in clay soil.
- Early start to the season due to warmer soil.
- Longer growing season due to warmer soil.
- Less soil erosion.
- More room for growth.
- Human foot traffic does not compress the soil.

Square Foot Gardening

This method is most useful if you're short on space. A deep raised bed is divided into 1-foot modules, and each crop is planted in one of these modules. Salad crops and small vegetables greatly benefit from this technique. Planting crops close to one another creates a microclimate that makes it hard for weeds to grow. Plus, the crops can easily be reached from all sides, making it a highly convenient method to raise your own food just outside your kitchen window.

Benefits of Square Foot Gardening

Square foot gardening offers many benefits, and some of them are:

It's easy to create: Even for novices, building a square foot garden is a straightforward process. It's a raised bed gardening technique that can be used anywhere because the bed is portable. You could build your square foot garden anywhere: on the ground, on the sidewalk, on a balcony, or on a terrace, for example. A square foot garden can be built in a few hours.

It is very efficient for high production: Square foot gardening is a high-yielding gardening method that uses little space to create large harvests. If you're short on space in your garden, this is the ideal option for you. In a smaller area, you'll have a better chance of growing more veggies or fruits.

It's cheap to maintain: Compared to other types of gardens, a square foot garden has less maintenance cost. There are fewer plants to buy, plant, and harvest since the garden is small. You don't even have to put in extra effort in the yard. And cages or garden cloches make it easy to protect small areas against pests and temperature fluctuations.

There is no overplanting: Overplanting won't be an issue with square foot gardening. It helps gardeners concentrate their efforts on a few plants that are absolutely necessary. Normal gardening produces a lot of crops that gardeners may simply throw away if the crops are bad.

Is Square Foot Gardening Cost-Effective?

Raised beds are a costly part of square foot gardening. It's expensive to fill the raised bed with soilless potting mix. You can lose a lot of money if you're not careful.

KEY TAKEAWAYS

Five methods you could consider when planning your vegetable garden are:

- Traditional vegetable garden
- Permaculture
- No-dig
- Raised beds
- Square foot garden

---

1. Don't even bother since we are going organic!

4

DIY ORGANIC WAY

Remember the reason you first began this journey? Of course, it wasn't because you wanted to brag to your neighbor about your new garden[1]. Instead, you began this journey because you wanted to GO ORGANIC! You wanted to follow nature's rules to please Mother Earth. You wanted to do away with artificial fertilizers, and, trust me, you've come so far and you're well on your way to becoming who you want to be. Can you imagine the joy in your soul? Can you imagine your backyard full of green veggies? All these will be yours, but only if you truly follow what it takes to grow an organic garden.

But more than all these, have you ever asked yourself this question—**why go organic?** Why do you really want to use soil naturally?

When I was younger, one of the many things my mother taught me was always to have a reason for anything I do because this would boost my morale on days when I feel like giving up. So, right now, I want you to think about why you really want to go organic.

In my answer to this same question, I came up with some reasons that pushed me into organic farming, and I'll surely share them with you. *Just stick around.*

WHY DO YOU WANT TO GROW YOUR FOOD ORGANICALLY?

One of the many reasons for going organic is that organic gardening is healthier for us, our community, and our environment. Also, organic gardeners use natural supplies, cultural practices, and biological processes in the garden, that is to say, synthetic chemicals are completely avoided. But that's just the tip of the iceberg; other reasons are:

- **Organic farming yields the most nutritious food.**

Organic products supply the body with enough nutritious food. Yes, I know that more than sweetness, what your body thirsts for is nutritional food, and that can be found in, guess where - organic garden products! Also, to grow nutritious veggies and fruits, the best organic gardens use rich, healthy soil, instead of chemical plant food. In the end, all this means one thing, organic soil is rich in soil nutrients and will give your body enough nutrition too.

- **Going organic is becoming a friend to the environment.**

Organic farming methods help to preserve our soil. The act of using fertilizers and chemicals will automatically record you in the book of nature haters. And more than being Mother Earth's friend, you are also fighting climate change. Also, since organic gardens lack inorganic materials like pesticides, they are safe for pets, children, and the general public to enjoy. You don't have to start thinking about taking your pet to the vet just because they saunter in your garden.

- **By going organic, you get to learn more about nature.**

When you feed and preserve your garden veggies naturally, you'll learn about the natural world's workings over time. Also, once you have begun to learn the natural materials you are dealing with, it will help you to know more about nature, and this includes what to plant, when to plant, and how to plant it. Like it's been said - **Knowledge is Power.**

- **It makes the soil healthy.**

The foundation of every successful organic farm is healthy soil. An organic soil uses practices such as crop rotation to improve the advantages of the soil. That is, with organic farming, you can fully reach the potential of your soil and regain the quality it possesses just like the first time you started working on it.

So, voila!

Knowing all this, I remind myself why I went into organic farming whenever I feel like giving up. Most importantly, another reason to go into organic farming is to avoid health problems caused by chemicals used to treat food – problems like obesity, cancer, heart disease, high blood pressure, and diabetes. Knowing all this will help you know the risks of eating non-organic food.

ADVERSE EFFECTS OF NON-ORGANIC FOODS

Eating non-organic food has a slew of health risks, like the laying of pollutants and toxic substances' foundation in the body, which can lead to a host of other problems. So, you have to be really careful about what you eat as fresh food.

Even though the inorganic way of producing food seems like a big blessing to humanity as we have gone far in technology, and offers a faster and more efficient way to manufacture food, the truth is that it can have a negative impact on customers any day, anytime.

You should never forget that over the years, we have now doubled the rate at which we use chemicals to grow our plants and produce our food. All these have excluded the viewpoint of organic gardens. Truth is, agricultural chemicals have become more important in our food production and the painful part also is that, the more the chemicals, the more people use them.

By eating processed meals, you are literally injecting chemicals into your body. Manufacturers process food with chemicals to make it last longer. You should also note that when you eat processed food, you're also eating antibiotics, pesticides, and hormones. Also, don't forget the genetically modified organisms. You know, GMOs are another dangerous byproduct of the process of transferring specific traits or genes from one organism to a different plant or animal. Eating organic is just the better way for several reasons, and never forget that your health is the most important one.

Contamination by pesticides is a major problem in inorganic farming. Adding chemicals into agriculture also reduces soil and greatly threatens biodiversity. Nutritious soil is essential for growing healthy food! You want yummy? Go healthy.

Pesticides and herbicides can affect our health negatively. It has been revealed that pesticide exposure can cause neurotoxicity, reproductive outcomes, malignancies, dermatologic impacts, and respiratory disorders such as asthma (beware of those health-threatening and teeth breaking terms). Most organizations recommend we reduce the use of pesticides. Would you like to know another shocking fact? Another thing to know is that pesticides are harmful to people; so, they must be handled carefully and thrown away properly. While organic farming disposes of pesticides in a way that doesn't pollute our environment, conventional farming does not. Eat organic if you want to avoid pesticides because conventionally grown food often includes pesticide residue.

Agriculture contributes to greenhouse gas[2] emissions in many ways, including deforestation for farming, methane gas emissions from animals, and the use of nitrogen fertilizers (which is commonly found in non-organic agriculture). Non-organic farms emit more greenhouse gasses and use more energy than organic farms do. Organic farming reduces greenhouse gas emissions by increasing soil carbon absorption and using less synthetic nitrogen fertilizers. Studies have shown that organic farming uses less energy, pollutes the land less, and emits fewer greenhouse gases.

One of the main adverse effects of non-organic farming is emulsifiers. Emulsifiers are used to improve food texture and shelf life. They may be found in different foods, from margarine to ice cream and even bread. Emulsifiers, according to most research, can alter gut microbes. This inflammation is usually linked to both Crohn's disease and inflammatory bowel disease (IBD).

Knowing these adverse effects of non-organic farming will show you why organic farming is the better system and the only natural solution to some of the problems plaguing the earth. Knowing the differences between these two systems will help you appreciate organic farming better.

ORGANIC AND NON-ORGANIC FARMING IN DIFFERENT SITUATIONS

The difference between organic and inorganic food confuses most people. What you eat is essential to your health. Organic food is more nutritious than conventionally grown food. This is because it is produced with the assistance of Mother Nature, rather than man. However, chemicals, pesticides, and herbicides are used to grow non-organic food, all of which are dangerous to our health. There are many health risks linked to eating non-organic food. When food is treated with chemicals, traces of the chemicals remain in the food, even after it has been thoroughly cooked. These residues affect our organs and disturb our body's natural functions.

To understand this better, here are a few differences between organic and inorganic farming:

- **In the use of pesticides.**

Farmers strive to produce greater harvests because they've invested so much money in their farm. But, most times, they might not achieve the estimated crop yield due to insect pests. Insects eat up and stunt the growth of crops. Farmers may then use chemicals on their fields to kill these insects. If you don't wash your food properly before cooking and eating it, traces of pesticides could settle in your body and make you sick. With organic farming, there are traditional ways to get rid of insects. It is your responsibility to ensure that you and your family eat organic food in order to live longer and healthier.

- **In processed foods.**

In industrialized nations, processed meals are becoming popular since they take less time to prepare. However, it is risky to rely completely on processed meals. When you're preparing yourself for work or your children for school, you might want to pack processed food since it will save you a lot of time. However, there are many phases in food processing where the food's nutrient level is reduced, so processed food isn't nutritious.

Adding more salt, sugar, sodium, oil, and spices to food can make the food taste unnatural. Food loses its nutritional value when it is cooked, and adding too much salt, sugar, or sodium doesn't help. Avoiding meals that have too many non-organic ingredients will lead to a healthier lifestyle.

Pregnant women should eat only healthy food. During pregnancy, every woman knows that she needs to eat organic food. Still, she might crave non-organic food. If she eats non-organic food without knowing, she might suffer terrible problems, like fetal failure. What's more, pesticide exposure is bad for fetal growth, which is an important stage in every child's development.

After learning these adverse effects of non-organic farming, you might be wondering, **"What, then, are the benefits of organic farming/food?"**

Organic food has so many benefits, and I'll explain some of them in the next section.

BENEFITS OF EATING ORGANIC VEGETABLES

You should know that the way you plant your food can affect your mental and emotional health as well as the environment. For example, people who are sensitive to food, chemicals, or preservatives may find that eating solely organic food lessens or treats their symptoms. After all, organic food contains essential elements (like antioxidants), unlike conventionally grown food. Here are some benefits of eating organic vegetables:

- **Organic vegetables don't have pesticides.**

In traditional agriculture, chemicals like synthetic fungicides, herbicides, and insecticides are normally used to treat plants, so some of them remain in and on the food we eat. Organic farming does not use any of these chemicals.

- **Organic vegetables don't have GMOs.**

Organic food is GMO-free, which means it isn't genetically modified in a lab or processed (I know you get what I mean). The use of genetic modification in food is pretty bad for your health. Simple. Oh! you need an example, picture this: to increase resistance to pesticides and herbicides, foods and plants have their DNA changed in ways that don't occur naturally. Food safety activists are worried as there isn't enough research to say how safe GMOs are, even if there isn't enough data to say how unsafe they are.

- **It helps with heart problems.**

The amount of conjugated linoleic acid in animal products would increase if animals graze only on natural grass. This is because natural grass absorbs the sun's energy through photosynthesis and converts it into the most desired organic product for animals who eat it. So, natural grass is a heart-healthy fatty acid that can improve heart protection, and it is found in higher concentrations in the meat and milk products of free-range animals.

- **Organic food builds a stronger immune system.**

The main goal of organic and inorganic gardening methods is to do whatever it takes to boost agricultural productivity. Using inorganic materials, for example, the idea of increasing the production of grains, meat, fruits, and vegetables seems to tackle some of the world's food security issues. But there are serious consequences that aren't so obvious, like an increased risk of allergies and a weaker immune system. Because organic food is not altered in any way, eating it reduces the risk of hurting your immune system. What's more, organic food has more vitamins and minerals, which helps improve our immune system.

- **You don't have to worry about foodborne diseases.**

Lately, the news has recorded many cases of foodborne diseases. Eggs, spinach, peanut butter, melons, and fast food are at the top of the list since their production is mainly focused on agricultural profits. Many animals are treated, vaccinated, and given animal by-products to make their products meet customer demands, which can make them sick. This technique is known as CAFOs (concentrated animal feeding operations) because it causes deadly drug-resistant illnesses to end-users when they eat food gotten from the animal. Organic food is the most effective way to avoid outbreaks of foodborne diseases.

If you want to enjoy organic farming, you must also use organic fertilizer. Organic fertilizer made from natural sources is nothing new. People grow vegetables in their garden that are healthier, cheaper, and better-tasting than the ones sold at the market. The foundation of a great garden is rich soil. The answer is to use natural fertilizer such as organic waste, compost, and homemade plant food. Making your own natural organic homemade fertilizer is cheap and easy. Usually, you would have to use household items. You could make your own organic fertilizer from plant or animal leftovers or leftover food and grass clippings [3].

HOW TO MAKE ORGANIC FERTILIZER

Creating your own organic homemade fertilizer from scratch is simple and fun; plus, the results are amazing. Most people know that the most effective way to improve garden soil is to add compost to it. Leftover food and grass clippings can be used as compost, saving you a lot of money. The essence of all these is making sure that you are sticking with the organic gardening rules.

So, if you want to grow vegetables at home, composting may be all you need. Even if your soil is rich in nutrients, you may need to fertilize it if you're growing a more difficult vegetable garden. So, instead of artificial fertilizer to boost the growth of your vegetable like an inorganic farmer, you can make your own homemade fertilizer with just a little guidance.

Plant-based fertilizers include:

- Compost
- Seaweed
- Wood ash
- Alfalfa meal
- Cottonseed meal
- Soybean
- Kelp
- Banana

Animal-based fertilizers contain:

- Fish emulsion from fish parts
- Fish meal
- Blood meal
- Cow manure and steer manure
- Bat guano
- Worm castings
- Bone meal

- **Making Fertilizer from Bananas**

Bananas are not only tasty and nutritious for us, but they also help several plants. First, bury a banana (or simply the peel) in the hole alongside the plant before planting it. Then, bury more bananas or banana peels into the top layer of soil as the plant grows. Both of these methods will give your plants the potassium they need to grow well.

Organic Banana Peels Recipe

- As you've read, banana peel contains enough potassium that will supply your plant with adequate green growth.
- Before planting, bury the banana peels. If you want to go deep organic, bury it under mulch to allow it to compost. This will quicken the soil fertility and will result in your plants blooming big.
- Tip for roses: add Epsom salt to give your big bloom rose a vibrant color. Others will think it was edited with Photoshop when you show them the picture of your happy, blooming rose.

- **Making Fertilizer from Blackstrap Molasses**

Many important plant nutrients are found in blackstrap molasses, including carbon, iron, sulfur, potash, calcium, manganese, potassium, copper, and magnesium. This fertilizer is good because it feeds beneficial bacteria, which keep the soil and plants healthy. Mix blackstrap molasses with another all-purpose fertilizer to use as a fertilizer. For example, 1 cup each of Epsom salts and alfalfa meal is an excellent combo to use. Combine this mixture with 4 gallons of water and 1 tablespoon of blackstrap molasses. You could also combine blackstrap molasses with compost tea. But do this only after brewing the compost tea.

- **Making Fertilizer from Manure**

Manure is produced by many animals, including cows, horses, chickens, and even bats. Each form of manure is rich in nitrogen and other nutrients, but it must be used carefully. Raw manure is very acidic and may contain more nutrients than your plants need to grow, so too much of it might burn them. It is better to use composted manure. Since it's less nutrient-dense and less acidic, you may apply more of it to increase water retention in your soil without hurting your plants. You won't have to wait long since manure decomposes quickly into a wonderful odor-free soil additive.

Organic Manure Recipe

- Get a bowl of decayed goat, chicken, cow, or horse manure. You can ask your neighbor who rears these animals. Trust me, to them it is a smelling substance but to you it is worth millions.
- For the best result, use old cow shit!
- Now, fill it in an old cloth that can serve as a sieve.
- Keep it cool and dry for 3–4 days.
- Later on, you can add this manure to the soil. Bury your fabrics or throw them away. Everything will work for the good of your organic garden.

- **Making Fertilizer from Fallen Tree Leaves**

Instead of bagging up your fallen leaves and tossing them out on the curb, collect them for your gardening. Leaves have many trace minerals; they also attract earthworms, which keep your soil moist and lighten heavy soil. You could use leaves two ways: plow them into your soil (or put crushed leaves into potting soil) or use them as mulch to nourish your plants while also keeping weeds at bay.

- **Making Fertilizer from Coffee Grounds**

While coffee grounds have many uses, their finest application is as a fertilizer. Several plants like acidic soil, including blueberries, rhododendrons, roses, and tomatoes. Recycling your coffee grounds will make your soil more acidic. You could either treat your garden by scattering used coffee grounds on top of the soil, or you could brew "coffee" to pour on your plants. Then, use the water to irrigate your acid-loving plants after soaking up to 6 cups of old coffee grounds in it for at least a week.

Organic Coffee Ground Recipe

- Tomatoes, blueberries, and roses benefit from the nitrogen in coffee grounds.
- Sprinkle the coffee powder on top of your soil. It will help your plants grow well.
- Mix 6 cups of coffee grinds in 5 gallons of water.
- Let the mixture settle for 4 days.

- **Making Fertilizer from Eggshells**

Don't ever forget this—eggshells are a useful fertilizer because of the little amounts of nitrogen present. In order to grow your plant properly, you must know that most roots need a small amount of calcium near their growing tips. This is a great way to "recycle" your eggshells since plant development reduces soil calcium levels, and calcium is essential. Use a coffee grinder to crush eggshells into a fine powder, then scatter the powder over your garden soil.

- **Making Fertilizer from Wood Ash**

You may add potassium and calcium carbonate to your soil by using ashes. Hardwood is ideal, but please don't use charcoal or lighter fluid around your plants since it might hurt them. Likewise, avoid using ash in areas with acid-loving plants since ashes are alkaline and can increase the soil's alkalinity.

SIMPLE TIPS TO FOLLOW IF YOU WOULD LIKE TO MAKE ORGANIC FERTILIZER

This is mainly for the compost tea recipe:

- Fill a gallon bucket one-third with good compost that you have made.
- Pour water in a bucket to the brim.
- Give the content (the compost and water) 4 days' time.
- Then, stir the mixture gently.
- Strain the mixture with any old fabric that has little tiny holes. (This will allow the water to pass through)
- Now, you can pour the leftover compost into your garden.
- Mix the remaining water fertilizer with water (not too much.)
- Now, get your sprayer, pour it inside, and spray on your leaves.

THEN, WATCH THE ORGANIC FERTILIZER PERFORM A MIRACLE.

SO, WHAT ABOUT COMPOST?

As an organic farmer, you must add compost to your soil after each planting season if you want to improve the quality of your soil even more. Compost is rich in nutrients, and it encourages the growth of beneficial soil microorganisms that help plants. Compost is simply organic materials that have decayed. When organic waste like leaves and vegetable scraps are composted, a rich soil blend known as black gold is created.

What is compost?

Compost is organic material that has decomposed, such as leaves, grass clippings, and kitchen trash. Because it contains many important minerals for plant development, it is normally used as a fertilizer. Compost also contains the right amounts of moisture, nutrients, and air, which can help improve soil structure. Also, it improves the texture of both clay and sandy soils, making them rich, moisture-retaining, and loamy. One of nature's greatest mulches and soil additives is compost. Most gardeners understand the importance of this rich, dark, earthy substance in enriching the soil and providing a healthy habitat for plants.

How can you compost your garden?

Compost may be bought in bags, but the best source is homemade compost. Compost, like homemade soup, varies based on the materials used, and there is no unique list of elements to produce a decent result. Common ingredients are fruit and vegetable scraps, old vegetable plants, fallen leaves, and grass clippings.

Why should you even bother about compost?

Compost aids the soil food web, which is made up of tiny bacteria and fungi as well as earthworms, crickets, and other organisms. Plant roots and many fungi develop symbiotic or mutually beneficial relationships, allowing vegetables to better sustain themselves. Compost has been shown to boost not only the disease resistance of tomatoes and other crops, but also their flavor and nutritional value. Compost also keeps the soil moist. What's more, composting will help your garden produce more healthy plants and less waste.

Common issues with compost:

- If the compost pile doesn't heat up, add more greens; water and aeration may be needed.
- Turn the compost or add brown stuff to dry it out if it smells like ammonia or rotten eggs.
- Dropped apples and kitchen leftovers might attract wasps and other pests, so stir the compost pile more often if necessary.

Never ever compost these things:

- Meat, seafood, and animal fats—they can attract pests to your compost pile.
- Compostable materials such as newspaper

shreds or office paper—they may add harmful chemicals to your compost. Instead of wasting them, recycle them.

- Grill ashes—wood ashes can be very useful in small quantities, but BBQ grill ashes should NEVER be composted.
- Dog and cat feces—they can infect your compost and smell bad. Consider using manures from different animals, instead of just cows or rabbits.
- Toxic chemicals—they are sometimes used to treat timber, which results in the creation of sawdust.

Composting requires nitrogen-rich "greens", carbon-rich "browns", water, and air. Greens include fresh grass clippings, coffee grounds/filters, tea bags, plant trimmings, fruit and vegetable leftovers, and eggshells. Dead plants, sawdust from untreated timber, twigs, dried grasses, weeds, straw, and leaves are examples of browns. Water decomposes the material and helps compost microorganisms thrive. Make sure the compost is wet before adding any organic material to it. Air aids decomposition so that bad smell won't be overwhelming. Ideally, the ratio of greens to browns should be 1:4.

ORGANIC METHODS THAT WILL HELP YOU CONTROL PESTS AND DISEASES

Every gardener faces pest infestation when starting or growing a garden. If pests manage to get into your flowers or veggies, don't allow them to set up shop there. Some of the best ways to deal with them are:

- **Neem Oil**

When it comes to organic pest management, neem oil[4] is a gardener's best friend. Neem oil has been used for over a century and is derived from the neem tree's leaves and seeds. Neem affects different insects in different ways, depending on the insect's age and genetic makeup. It works as an antifeedant, which means it reduces the pest's urge to feast on your delicate lettuce plants. Also, it can choke insects by covering them with a thin layer of material. Finally, neem can affect insect hormones, preventing pests from maturing, thus interrupting their breeding cycle.

- **Row Covers**

Isolating plants during their most vulnerable stages is one of the most efficient ways to keep pests out of your garden. Row covers can keep hungry pests at bay long enough for your plants to become stronger and less appealing to them. When choosing a material for row covers, choose lightweight materials that provide enough ventilation and sunlight exposure for plant development. Remember that investing time and money into row covers can extend your growing season by protecting your plants from frost in the late autumn and early spring.

If you want to treat fungal infections, mildew, or rust, combine 0.5 ounces of bicarbonate of soda with 1.5 ounces of soap flakes in 4 cups of hot water. Then, cool and strain it before spraying it on your plants. Alternatively, you could make a spray out of milk and water in a 1:2 ratio and spray your plants with it.

Encourage the presence of beneficial insects like ladybugs, honey bees, and ground beetles in your garden. Buy them if you have to (many are available commercially at the time of year they are needed).

WHAT DOES IT MEAN TO BE ORGANIC?

You can't use artificial products in organic farming. Even though, while it's true that we've gotten used to natural disasters, we've also had less trial and error to uncover new risks. Even if it were possible, it's often hard to tell whether something is natural or manufactured. Your idea of what's natural might differ from another person's idea, so there is no hard and fast rule. Over the years, the thin line between natural and artificial has sparked a lot of debate among farmers.

KEY TAKEAWAYS

- There are many benefits to being an organic farmer and food consumer.
- You can make homemade fertilizer, which gives you varieties of organic fertilizers.
- Adding compost to your soil will nourish it.

---

1. You don't have to worry, because they will see it.
2. A greenhouse gas (GHG or GhG) is a gas that absorbs and emits radiant energy within the thermal infrared range, causing the greenhouse effect.
3. Grass clippings are the cut grasses that are left behind or captured in a grass catcher by your mower when you cut your lawn.
4. Neem oil, also known as margosa oil, is a vegetable oil pressed from the fruits and seeds of the neem.

5

BEST VEGGIES AND HERBS FOR EASE AND HAPPINESS

A garden is not regarded as one if there is nothing there. What do I mean by this? Imagine this—you picked up this book, read about ways you can plant organically, types of organic farming, and more. But, you didn't see me mention the best veggies and herbs you can have in your garden. That's totally inconsiderate, right? Of course, it is! Like I said when we both began this journey, I am here to guide you through this; meanwhile, all you need to do is continue flipping through the pages while you note the important points I am telling you. Don't skim through the pages; stick around with me.

But before I start, let me give you a sneak peek of what you will learn in this chapter, *all because you have been a faithful reader (insert a grinning emoji).* So, in this chapter, you will be learning about... Wait! Have you been thinking about where to begin? Or are you wondering about the best vegetables to start with? I mean, you want to start seeing the fruitfulness of your garden, I know. This is why I have carefully worked on this chapter, to provide you with the best kind of veggies and herbs for your ease and happiness. So, what next? Let's jump right in!

THE GROWING STARTER PACK FOR EASY VEGETABLES AND HERBS

Before I start, note this: you don't have to worry about these vegetables; they are all that you are familiar with —oh yeah, I bet you are!

- **Chives**

Have you been waiting to see which plant will be first on the list? Do you think it's a coincidence that it's chives? Let me tell you about chives if you're interested —of course, I know you are. Chives will thrive in a random area of dirt in your landscape, as well as in a raised bed or a container. They are even grown indoors. Chives can quickly take over a garden, so you'll need to divide them every 3 to 4 years if you want your other plants to have a chance to grow. However, due to their pleasant flavor, they are becoming increasingly popular as garden additions. Apart from their garlicky aroma, chives have a number of health benefits that are worth learning about.

To grow your chives, follow these instructions closely to get the best result.

Chive seeds should be sown in a plastic container. This plant requires temperatures ranging from 20 to 25 degrees Celsius to germinate, therefore use a heated propagator or place on a warm windowsill. Within three weeks, seedlings should develop. Unless your pot is really crowded, there's no need to trim them out. When your seedlings reach around 5cm in height, remove them from the propagator and transplant them into 15-20 cm (6–8 inch) pots of peat-free multipurpose compost. Grow these young seedlings in colder circumstances, hardening them off for approximately a week before putting them outside.

- Although chives are drought resistant, constant irrigation throughout the growing season is essential for optimum yields. When watering, fully moisten the soil.
- Because the tiny bulbs of chives grow near the soil's surface, apply mulch to preserve moisture and keep weeds at bay.

- If your soil isn't already nutrient-rich, top-dress with a nitrogen-heavy fertilizer in late spring or early summer to boost yield.
- After the blooms have bloomed, remove them to prevent the seeds from spreading over your garden.
- Chives are significantly more prolific when split on a regular basis.
- Put them into clusters of at least 10 tiny bulbs and let them develop for several weeks before harvesting.

- **Lettuce**

Lettuce is a member of the cruciferous family as well. You don't have to be concerned because it thrives in practically any environment. This includes cold spots with direct sun exposure as well as shaded areas in hotter climates. It is common practice to thin lettuce in order for it to grow larger and taste better. You don't have to do this, though. It will grow with almost no effort on your side (it only needs watering twice a week). It's pointless to explain how to eat lettuce. In any case, it's delicious and has a fairly sweet flavor that everybody can appreciate. Lettuce contains vitamin K, which helps to build bones. Consuming enough vitamin K can help lower your risk of bone fracture.

Because lettuce has short roots, it requires regular watering. At least twice a week, check the soil and water if it is dry down to 1 inch deep. Lettuce containers require more regular watering than garden beds, especially in the summer. Surround the plant with about 2 to 3 inches of mulch. Mulch prevents weed growth by limiting sunlight, keeping soil wet, and keeping lettuce clean. Regular fertilizer feedings, in addition to good soil, will promote the optimum development from your lettuce.

- Plant lettuce in the early spring and late fall when the temperature is moderate. This healthy, leafy green is ideal for in-ground gardening, raised garden beds, and container gardening.
- Plant lettuce plants 6 to 18 inches apart (depending on type) in a sunny location with rich, well-drained soil with a pH between 6.0 and 7.0.
- Mix across several inches of old compost to improve native soil.
- To ensure delicate leaves, keep moisture levels consistent by watering anytime the top inch of soil becomes dry.
- Apply a thick layer of mulch made from finely crushed leaves or bark to prevent

weeds and help your watering efforts last longer.

- Feed a water-soluble plant food on a regular basis to encourage great leaf development.
- When the leaf lettuce is grown enough to consume, start with the outermost leaves and work your way in.

- **Green Onions**

The next on the list is green onions. What's nice about green onions is that you can grow your own from the onions you buy at the supermarket. Simply place the white bottoms in a cup of water on a shelf, with just a bit of green over the water. You'll get fresh green tops in a couple of days. Replace the water every few days (*newsflash:* if you don't, it will become disgusting). You can keep them running like this for weeks, if not months, but I think they lose flavor after a while. Growing the onions you've been regrowing in water in soil seems to restore their grocery-store splendor. Green onions offer several digestive advantages. Green onions' fiber content aids your body in maintaining a high number of good microorganisms. As a result, many individuals serve green onions as appetizers. The most significant aspect of green onions is that they are rich in vitamins and other necessary elements.

Plant onion seedlings as soon as the soil is workable in the spring. Onion seeds germinate in soil temperatures ranging from 65° F to 86° F. Plant the seed, cover with ½ of soil, and maintain wetness. Before planting outside, you can maintain them for 6-8 weeks inside. They can be spaced approximately 1-2" apart in the garden. Simply push onion sets into the soil approximately 2" apart to plant. Onions thrive in full sun, soil pH of 6.0-7.5, and well-drained soil with lots of premium compost or well-rotted manure. During the growth season, apply a full balanced fertilizer.

- **Arugula**

Arugula is a vegetable that people either admire or despise. Some people dislike its musky odor and flavor, while others find its peppery burn quite refreshing. Arugula is a green vegetable with uneven, lobed leaves that are delicate and tasty while young but get bitter as they age. The flavor is described as peppery or mustardy, and the leaves are frequently used raw in salads, as a garnish on sandwiches, or in stir-fries or soups. Nicole Burke, the founder of Gardenary, says, "Arugula grows very easily from seed." It is rich in nutrients such as vitamin K, vitamin A, vitamin C and minerals like calcium, potassium, and manganese. According to Burke, this gives it a nutritional profile similar to kale, though it is simpler to grow. It's also not very large, making it ideal for patios and tiny spaces—it'll happily thrive in a little pot. Arugula is rich in antioxidants, which are chemicals that help prevent or reverse cell damage. These natural chemicals, which give arugula its bitter taste and pungent fragrance, can protect you from diseases like cancer of the breast, prostate, lung, or colon. Arugula can also help to reduce inflammation. What's more, it has a lot of vitamin K, which is healthy for your bones and can help you avoid fractures.

Arugula grows best in a good soil, but it prefers a lot of moisture, so, follow this rule and get the best results - **water often**. The plants also like a pH range of 6 to 6.5 in their soil. To meet both of these requirements, dig in some well-rotted manure or compost before planting. This should be done as soon as the soil can be worked in the spring, or better yet, in the autumn before you close down your beds so they're ready to plant in the spring. Arugula prefers cold weather and may be planted as early as April in most regions of the United States. All you need are temperatures over 40 degrees Fahrenheit during the day (4 degree Celsius). Even frost won't stop it. Arugula grows best in full sun, but it may take moderate shade.

- **Parsley**

Parsley is easy to grow outside (it thrives in 8-inch-diameter containers). It grows abundantly and tastes delicious—as long as you plant it in the right season for your hardiness zone. Burke explains that the issue with parsley is seeing it as a spring and autumn plant rather than a summer one. "Grow it in colder weather," she recommends. When it comes to temperature, the plant might be cranky. For the same reason, it's hard to bring it indoors, so enjoy this herb during its growing season, and then switch to dried parsley in summer and winter. Parsley plants are tolerant to many conditions. They will thrive in situations ranging from full sunlight to partial shade. If your growing region is very hot, midday shade will be great—though the plants should get at least 8 hours of sunlight per day. Parley is a trustworthy warrior in the fight against cancer. By this, I mean that it has the potential to increase your body's cancer-fighting ability. Parsley has several vitamins, minerals, and antioxidants that could benefit your health. For example, it has a high concentration of vitamin K.

Plant parsley seedlings straight into your mulched soil, 1cm deep and 30cm apart, in rows 1cm apart. Cover the seeds lightly with water and thoroughly soak them. Thin seedlings to 15cm apart when they are large enough. If you have less room, fill a container with seed compost and thinly plant seeds, covering with a light layer of compost and wetting it. Make certain that the compost does not dry out. Seeds can take up to six weeks to germinate and should be thinned out and potted as soon as they are large enough. To keep the young plants from drying out when transplanting to a larger container, use a combination of garden and soil-based compost. Sow seeds in groups a few weeks apart to ensure a steady supply of parsley.

- **Basil**

Basil may be grown in spring or summer. Why? Because most people seem to enjoy it, and planting things that you will enjoy eating is crucial. You may even save yourself the trouble of growing one from seed by buying a tiny basil plant from a nursery instead. Basil can be grown inside all year, although it is more difficult. Basil is quite happy in a pot outside (a 12-inch-deep pot is considered ideal, but it can thrive in smaller pots), but it might need a grow light indoors. Basil is rich in vitamins, minerals, and antioxidants, including lutein, zeaxanthin, beta-carotene, and beta-cryptoxanthin. Basil's antioxidants and oils are responsible for many of its health benefits. Unfortunately, these substances are largely lost during the drying process, so use fresh basil if you want to fully enjoy its benefits.

Planting basil is simple. It grows best in wet, well-drained soil. If you have any compost or fertilizer on hand, add it to the soil to help your basil grow. If you're growing basil in a pot, make sure to flip it every couple of weeks to ensure even growth. Planting basil 2 weeks after the last spring frost is recommended. This aromatic herb is ideal for raised garden beds, containers, and in-ground gardening. Basil should be spaced according to the label's instructions, which are generally 12 to 18 inches apart. Grow in well-drained, rich soil with a pH of 6.0 to 7.0. Consider using a high-quality bagged potting mix for container gardening. Basil thrives on wet soil, so keep an eye on moisture levels and water deeply if the top inch of soil becomes dry. Pinch off the uppermost branches of basil plants when they reach 4 to 6 inches in height to encourage additional side shoots and a larger plant overall. To keep your plant from going to seed, nip off the flowers.

- **Oregano**

Don't fret. I wasn't going to skip it. I was saving the best it for the last. Growing oregano is easy. It may be planted from seeds, cuttings, or potted plants. Seeds should be sown indoors before the final predicted frost date in your area. It is not necessary to cover oregano herb seeds with dirt. Simply spray them with water and place them in a seed tray or container covered with plastic. Then, place it in a sunny area, such as a window, to help it grow. Within a week or so, the seeds generally germinate. When the plants reach about 6 inches (15 cm) in height, they can be trimmed to about a foot apart. Once the risk of frost has gone, it can be planted in the garden. Plant oregano in well-drained soil that gets enough sunlight. Oregano is a good source of Carvacrol, a chemical. Carvacrol has been used in ancient medicine for several health issues, and research shows that it has therapeutic advantages.

- **Radish**

Radish is a common root vegetable. It is also quite easy to grow, especially because it's one of the few plants that can be grown in small pots without difficulty. It is preferable to sow radish before summer so that it may spend the entire warm season growing underground.

Before the warm season begins, we recommend planting it in wet soil. Its flavor is nothing to be ashamed of. The crisp texture combined with the powerful taste is unmistakable. And, because of its rich purple color, radish has become a go-to pick for a visually appealing condiment to any meal. Because radish seeds are rather big, they are easy to plant and do not require thinning. Once planted, they'll be ready for harvest in a few weeks. The roots of the French breakfast radish are crisp, oval, red, and white, whereas those of the crimson globe radish have a brilliant scarlet color and white flesh.

Sow seeds 4–6 weeks before the average date of last frost for spring planting. To avoid disturbing the roots of radish plants, put them immediately in the garden. Sow seeds 1 inch deep and 1 inch apart in rows 12 inches apart outdoors. Plant another set of seeds every 10 days or so, while the temperature is still cold, for a steady supply of radishes in the late spring and early summer. Plan to plant in the fall. Radishes may be planted later than any other root crop in late summer or early fall and still yield a harvest. Sow seeds 4–6 weeks before the first frost of the season.

- **Bush Beans**

Bush beans thrive in well-drained, organic soil. However, to produce optimally, they need much sunlight. Bush beans also take more room than most of the plants on this list; they might use up a raised bed or a big container (check your bean variety for recommended depth). But depending on the variety of bush beans you're planting, you should see some results within 60 days. Bush beans don't attract as many pests as other fruiting plants, like tomatoes. Beans may be grown indoors in a container with a diameter of at least 8 inches and lots of sunshine. Its health benefits include regulating blood sugar levels, being a good source of fiber, improving heart health, reducing iron deficiency, possibly preventing cancer, boosting enzyme formation, being a good source of protein, preventing congenital disabilities, being a low-fat source, improving eye health, controlling premenstrual syndrome (PMS), caring for joints, and reducing depression.

Bush beans thrive on soil that is well-drained and rich in organic matter. They require full sun to produce optimally. Before you begin planting bush beans, you should consider inoculating the soil with bean inoculant, which contains bacteria that help the bean plant produce more. Your bush beans will still produce if you do not add bean inoculants to the soil, but it will help you get a larger crop from your bush beans. Plant bush bean seeds 1 1/2 inches (3.5 cm) deep and 3 inches (7.5 cm) apart. If you're planting more than one row of bush beans, space them 18 to 24 inches (46 to 61 cm) apart. Bush beans should germinate in one to two weeks.

- **Potato**

Potato is another underground plant that we can't ignore. Potatoes are easy to grow: put them in the ground or an old manure bag, cover the leaves with dirt when they first sprout (a process known as "earthing up"), and harvest them after a few weeks. Early potatoes (seeded in early April) can be gathered in July before the threat of potato blight increases. Red Duke of York potatoes are a lovely red-skinned variety, while Anya potatoes have lengthy tubers with a nutty flavor. Actually, we can't say enough nice things about them since they take little to no input to thrive. Potatoes grow in spring and are ready for harvest in summer. The majority of potatoes prefer somewhat chilly surroundings to warm ones. They also flourish in well-fertilized, nutrient-rich soil. You may eat potatoes however you like. Potatoes are always available to support your body with enough carbohydrates, whether you roast, bake, or boil them. Potatoes are one of the most common and most important foods globally, and they have a plethora of health benefits that make them even more important as a staple dietary item for most people. These health benefits include better digestive health, lower cholesterol levels, better heart health, protection against polyps, and better blood sugar control.

Potatoes are tubers, which are thickened subterranean stems. Potatoes require deep, loose, well-drained soil that is free of stones for proper tuber growth. They require direct sunlight. After the risk of severe frost has passed, plant tubers directly in the garden. Plant them in rows 2 feet apart, 2 to 3 inches deep, and 10 to 12 inches apart, with the eyes up. If the tops of growing tubers are exposed to sunshine, they will become green. Begin heaping soil around the base of the stems or surrounding the plants with a thick layer of mulch when the plants are approximately 5 to 6 inches tall. Throughout the growing season, potatoes require consistent irrigation.

Being an organic farmer also requires you to know how to plant these vegetables and herbs. And as I have said earlier, I will be teaching you everything you need to know about going organic all by yourself.

So, how can you plant these vegetables and herbs yourself?

Are you beginning to wonder how you are going to start growing my listed healthy vegetables and herbs? Trust me, as I have said earlier, I will be giving you everything you need to know about going organic and most importantly, how you can successively plant these plants. So, without wasting your time, I think - let's get started.

If I skip some varieties, and they grow in your area, don't worry, just plant them. You can find out what already grows in your region by speaking with a local gardener or nursery worker. Check around your environment and scout for those veggies and herbs that commonly grow in your area. Ask fellow gardeners. Knowing this can also give you ideas on which plant to bury[1] or which not to plant.

So, are you ready to plant one of the simplest vegetables to grow in your garden? If you choose one from the list above, you will avoid any unfavorable outcomes. Growing vegetables is not a difficult task. Though using any of these species will make your life easier, especially if you are usually busy or know very little about growing plants at home. What is certain is that you won't regret planting them. On the contrary, you'll be thrilled once you witness how a seed grows into a seedling, and finally into a full-grown veggie ready to be served at your table.

Over the years I've been an organic gardener, I have realized that we all want to feed ourselves and our family the healthiest meals. Know this—producing your own veggies ensures that you are eating the freshest food available. Paying attention to your soil and replenishing all vital trace elements is one way to enhance the nutritional value of your plants.

Now, the big question is: What are the healthiest veggies to plant in your garden?

HEALTHIEST VEGETABLES TO PLANT

Remember one of the famous lines written by George Orwell in his book[2]? "All animals are equal, but some animals are more equal than others." In the same way, **all veggies are rich in vitamins, minerals, and fiber. But some veggies stand out for their extraordinary health benefits.** Depending on their diets, general health, and nutritional demands, different veggies may benefit different people differently.

To answer the question I asked in the last section, I have compiled a list of some healthy vegetables that should never go far away from your plates, and here they are:

- **Spinach**

Because of its excellent nutritional content, this leafy green leads the list of the healthiest vegetables. One cup (30 grams) of raw spinach has 56% of your daily vitamin A needs, as well as your full daily vitamin K needs—all for only 7 calories. Spinach also has lots of antioxidants, which can help lower the risk of chronic illnesses. According to research, dark green leafy vegetables, like spinach, are rich in beta-carotene and lutein, two antioxidants that are known to reduce the risk of cancer. A 2015 study discovered that eating spinach can improve heart's health by lowering your blood pressure. Spinach contains a lot of iron, which is excellent for boosting energy and blood health. It's also rich in magnesium, which aids muscle and neuron function. If you use blood thinners like warfarin (Coumadin), you should exercise caution when eating dark leafy greens. For patients taking these medicines, doctors recommend taking a regular vitamin K dosage all the time.

- **Carrots**

Renowned American physician Michael Greger once said, "We should all be eating fruits and vegetables as if our lives depend on it—because they do." And I totally agree with him because what do you know about carrots? Carrots are rich in vitamin A, with 1 cup (128 grams) delivering 428 percent of the daily needed vitamin A dosage. Also, they contain beta-carotene, the antioxidant that gives them their bright orange color and can help prevent cancer. In fact, one study showed that for every serving of carrots eaten each week, the participants' risk of prostate cancer dropped by 5%. Another research found that eating carrots can help smokers lower their risk of lung cancer. Smokers who did not eat carrots at least thrice a week had a threefold increased risk of getting lung cancer as opposed to those who did. Carrots also contain a lot of vitamin C, vitamin K, and potassium. Finally, never forget this: they are beneficial to your eyes. This is probably the most popular carrot superpower. They're rich in beta-carotene, a compound that your body converts into vitamin A, which improves the health of your eyes. Furthermore, beta-carotene protects your eyes from the sun and reduces your risk of cataracts and other eye defects.

- **Broccoli**

Broccoli contains calcium, magnesium, and zinc, which helps alkalize the body and keep the bones healthy. It also contains vitamin A, which mends and smoothens collagen, as well as folate and iron, which help keep your blood healthy. Also, this super-healthy vegetable has anti-aging properties due to phytonutrients, fiber, and antioxidants, which help flush out pollutants. Just so you know, broccoli is a member of the cruciferous vegetable family. It is rich in glucosinolate, a sulfur-containing plant component, and sulforaphane, a by-product of glucosinolate. Sulforaphane is essential since it has been found to protect against cancer. Plus, sulforaphane was shown in animal research to lower the size and quantity of breast cancer cells while also inhibiting tumor development in mice. Eating broccoli can also help prevent various chronic illnesses. For example, according to a 2010 animal research study, eating broccoli sprouts can protect the heart from disease-causing oxidative stress by reducing oxidant levels.

- **Garlic**

Garlic contains allicin, a chemical related to its many health benefits. Garlic has been shown in studies to help control blood sugar and improve heart health. Garlic loses some of its nutritional value when cooked, so it's better to eat it raw. Garlic is an immune-system booster with several health benefits, including its ability to fight poisons and illnesses in the body. Garlic is beneficial to intestinal health. It contains components that, when digested, can aid in the development of beneficial bacteria, particularly lactobacillus. By decreasing free radical damage, it helps control the body's inflammatory response as well as the skin's capacity to combat inflammation.

- **Kale**

Kale is high in phytochemicals[3], plant protein, fiber, chlorophyll, minerals such as manganese, copper, calcium, potassium, folate, magnesium, phosphorus, iron, and folate, as well as vitamins A, B, C, E, and K, and even omega-3 fatty acids. Like other leafy greens, kale is well known for its health benefits, which include nutritional and antioxidant richness. A cup (67 g) of raw kale is rich in vitamin B, potassium, calcium, and copper. Finally, kale can be used to boost heart health due to its high antioxidant content.

- **Ginger**

Ginger root is used as a spice in a variety of recipes ranging from vegetables to desserts. Ginger has traditionally been used as a natural treatment for motion sickness. Several research has confirmed ginger's anti-nausea properties. In an analysis that was tried 12 times, ginger greatly reduced nausea in almost 1,300 pregnant women compared to a placebo. Ginger also has strong anti-inflammatory qualities, which can be used to treat inflammatory diseases such as arthritis, lupus, and gout. In one trial, participants with osteoarthritis who were given a concentrated ginger extract noticed a reduction in knee pain and relief from other symptoms.

- **Asparagus**

Asparagus is another excellent veggie to eat regularly. Asparagus stalks are low in calories but rich in fiber. Plus, they contain folate, vitamin C, vitamin A, and vitamin K. Asparagus has even been shown to protect the liver from poisons. Asparagus is a natural diuretic that helps to cleanse the digestive tract. It's also a good supply of plant-based amino acids and cofactors for various metabolic pathways in the body. You can meet a third of your daily folate needs by eating half a cup (90 grams) of asparagus. This quantity also contains a good amount of selenium, vitamin K, thiamin, and riboflavin.

- **Sweet Potato**

Sweet potatoes, which contain free-radical-fighting vitamins A and C, as well as carotenoids and beta-carotene, which the body converts to vitamin A, are delicious (and still nutritious!) starchy vegetables to add to your diet. They are also simple to prepare. Simply bake them at 425°F for 40 minutes, and you're done! If you're in the mood for something yummy, sprinkle on some salt (or a little cinnamon if you're in the mood for something sweet).

It's obvious that adding veggies to your diet is important to your health, from supplying important vitamins and minerals to fighting diseases. While the veggies listed below have been carefully researched for their health benefits, several others are just as healthy. So, make sure you're getting a decent variety of veggies in your diet to reap their many health benefits and get the most dietary value for your money.

But before I add the last period, don't ever forget these kitchen essentials for planting, such as:

- **Garlic**

Garlic belongs to the allium family. It is a bulbous vegetable that has been around for a long time. Garlic is easy to grow and takes up a little area in the yard. Garlic grows from individual cloves that break off a complete bulb. Each clove grows quickly in the soil, creating a new bulb with 5-10 cloves. Garlic is delicious when roasted or used as a seasoning in various dishes.

- **Onion**

Onions come in various sizes, shapes, colors, and flavors. But red, yellow, and white onions are the most popular varieties. Their flavors can range from sweet to harsh and from spicy to pungent, depending on the season they are grown and eaten in.

- **Potatoes**

Potatoes are rich in fiber, which can help you lose weight by keeping you full for a long time. Fiber can also help prevent heart diseases by maintaining healthy cholesterol and blood sugar levels. Potatoes are also rich in antioxidants, which help prevent diseases, as well as vitamins, which help your body function well.

- **Tomatoes**

Tomatoes are fruits, although they are mostly used as veggies in various recipes. They have high potassium and vitamin C content. What's more, lycopene and beta-carotene, both found in tomatoes, are known to lower the risk of cancer. Tomatoes also have chemicals that improve eye health.

KEY TAKEAWAYS

- Even though you want to start your own garden, you must start with healthy vegetables.
- To enrich your vitamins, grow the healthy vegetables.
- Finally, never forget the kitchen essentials.

---

1. Don't be scared, I am still talking about planting.
2. Animal Farm
3. Phytochemicals are chemical compounds produced by plants, generally to help them resist fungi, bacteria and plant virus infections

6

MAINTENANCE AND MORE

Do you feel tired a while after you start out?[1]

Let me give you a little pep talk.

One of the essential things in life is the ability to continue after you have started something. I remember one of my friends in college. He signed up for a workout class, and for the next two weeks, he was consistent with his 3-day workout plan. But afterward, he skipped the first day and rescheduled it for another day. But then he missed the second day, too, and also the third. And in the two years that followed, he never stepped into the gym again.

Janna Cachola, a New Zealand-based actress, singer, and model, once said, "Effort means nothing without consistency." For everything you start, you must maintain a drive that will take you further on days when you feel like giving up, and this drive is called consistency.

The essence of all this is to prepare you for the days you may not feel like working in your garden. Since your plants can't understand whether you are weak or stressed, or since you don't have enough knowledge yet, each attitude that does not fit into the nature of your organic garden will badly affect the plants.

This chapter will introduce you to affordable ways to grow your organic garden and still have an abundant harvest. These ways include pruning, mulching, watering, and so on.

AFFORDABLE WAYS TO MAINTAIN YOUR GARDEN

Plant care routines must be adjusted as the season changes. To help you understand this better, here is some valuable advice for the monsoon season and gardening suggestions for people who are just starting out their pastimes.

- **First, what is your budget?**

Study the size of your space and how much sunlight it gets, then use that information to decide which plants to grow. Also, think of how much space the plants will need in future. Will they grow to be too big for your garden space if you buy them as saplings? Get hanging planters, railing planters, and window boxes to make the most of your yard area. Lastly, choosing plants that are native to your location might make your life much easier because they will easily adapt.

- **Group the plants.**

Plants with similar needs should be grouped together. Plants like pothos, monstera, and Syngonium, for example, have similar needs, as do snake plants, aloe vera, peace lily, and ZZ plants. That way, you'll be able to recall which parts of your garden need little or more water. Label the pots if you're sowing seeds to make them easier to identify.

- **Control your pests.**

Keep in mind that not all insects are pests. Natural predators that kill or drive away undesirable insects include beneficial insects like honeybees and beetles. If you want the pests in your garden to see you as a samurai, try out these methods:

Methods

- Mix 2 tablespoons of neem oil with 1 teaspoon of mild liquid soap and 1 quart of water. Shake thoroughly before spraying on plants infested with garden pests.
- You can also try yellow sticky pads. They are affordable and widely available in local and online stores. You can use them to catch flies, aphids, and other pests around plants. Unfortunately for them, their bright color attracts bugs, which eventually get stuck on the pads and are unable to reach your plants.
- Make a paste with 500 grams each of green chilies, ginger, and garlic to treat infestations. Add 1 liter of water, then place it in a jar and leave it overnight. Spray this mix on the plants to repel insects.

- **Use plant labels for identification.**

Use slate labels to dress up your pots. By sticking labels to your pots, you'll never mix up your flowers again. Write the plants' names on small slate tiles using a white marker pen or chalk (if you would like to keep them as they are). Using pliers, bend the wire into rods with twisted hooks to hang them on. On the backside of the marker, write how often the plants need to be watered.

- **Use old kitchen utensils for your vegetable garden.**

If you want to make your garden more sustainable but don't have the money to plant a full-scale veggie patch, you could try a new vegetable trug. Marcus Eyles, horticultural director of Dobbies Garden Centres, proposes growing veggies from kitchen trash! "Spring onions and celery are two culinary staples that are easy to regenerate from their root base with a few inches of stem attached," he says. "Slice the stems, then set them to root down in a shallow glass of water. When new roots develop, put them in the garden to grow on." Next, collect the seeds of chilies and sweet peppers and plant them immediately into fresh compost. Finally, water them regularly and place them on a warm, sunny windowsill.

- **Use old cookware as planters.**

Before tossing out outdated cookware, consider whether they can be used as planters. Their tough skin makes them suitable for outdoor use. Before repotting your plants, just poke a few drainage holes at the bottom of the cookware.

- **Display your plants on an old ladder.**

Stylish ladder shelving can help you enhance your garden elements. These ladder racks are made by connecting two ladders at the top. Potted plants, lamps, and ornamental items are displayed on shelves made of wood boards put over the rungs. It's a cinch to create and a steal to buy – a positive step forward for low-budget gardening.

- **Turn that old kitchen cabinet into a potting table or farm tool chest.**

With a few simple changes, an old upright kitchen cabinet can be turned into a space to repot plants. Begin with a fresh coat of paint and consider replacing the worktop—in this case, a surface with a lip prevents soil from falling all over the floor. Install hooks on the side to hang shovels and other equipment for easy access. You could store compost, pots, seeds, and other items in it, saving up room in your shed.

- **Create a garden bar from the stuff in your basement.**

Picture this—you've just finished working in your garden, but instead of going inside your home, you sit in a cozy area you have created for relaxation, pour yourself a drink, and then relax. Can you imagine the feeling? So, set up a bar outside and make cocktail hour an outdoor experience instead of disappearing into the house every time you need a drink. You can get the supplies you need to build your own Tiki-style serving spot for a low cost from your local DIY store or bring in some old stuff from your basement, like chairs, shelves, or desks. You could also keep it simple and upcycle an old wooden bar cart, making sure to protect the wood from the weather. Packing a bucket with ice is all it takes to keep drinks cold!

- **Turn your garden shed into a summerhouse.**

You aren't making the most of your garden shed if all it does is store your toolbox and collect dust. You can easily transform it into a warm and inviting potting shed (unless you're handy with plants), a sunny summerhouse, a cool workshop, or even a garden playhouse for the kids.

Adding these leisure spots to your garden will make you more consistent with your garden. Now, picture this—you want to relax and have some fresh air. So, you go to the relaxation area in your garden and remember that you have not watered some of your flowers. The essence of all this is to make your gardening habits scale up so that you can be a good gardener.

Now, let us look at efficient ways to manage your garden vegetables.

MANAGING YOUR GARDEN

Effective Watering Techniques

Watering is useless if the water goes down the edge of the plants' base without reaching the roots. This might happen if you apply too much water at once or if you water too often. Watering slowly is usually more effective. The trick is to ensure that water reaches the roots, whether you're watering seedlings, houseplants, a row of tomatoes, or thirsty shrubs and trees.

It's also worth noting that 70-95 percent of most veggies are made up of water. To grow properly, they must collect nutrients from the soil and then transport those nutrients around the plant using water as a medium. As a result, a shortage of water will make your plants deficient in nutrients. So, watering your plants is important when managing a garden since a water shortage can influence the health of your plants.

So, here are some things you should note when it comes to watering your vegetables:

- **Know your soil.**

Soil is made up of various sized mineral particles (sand, silt, clay, rocks), organic matter (living and dead organisms), air, and water. It makes little difference if your soil is mostly sandy. However, it could also comprise all three particle sizes: sand, silt, and clay—all in various amounts. Why is this important? Clay-rich soil, such as mine, is denser and stores water for longer periods of time. Because clay soil retains moisture after rainfall and manual watering, you'll probably need to water your garden less often if you have it. But since water moves faster through sandy soil, it does not retain moisture for as long as clay-like soil. This means you'll have to water your plants more often and keep a closer eye on how soon the soil dries out.

- **Know the amount of water your vegetable can hold.**

Veggies, on average, need one inch of water each week. The total amount of water the garden gets—both from rain and from your watering—should be one inch. But keep in mind that your soil, not you, controls how much water it needs. Usually, you might get away with watering once a week if you have clay soil. If it rains one inch during that week, you won't need to water the garden anymore. The soil should keep the moisture from the recent rain very well! If you have sandy soil that does not retain moisture as well, you would most likely need to water more often. You could try watering the garden twice a week and giving it half an inch each time. Then, keep an eye on your plants' health and soil moisture to see whether that's enough.

- **You don't have to hoard watering - make it thorough.**

Drip irrigation is the cheapest way to irrigate your plant. But most gardeners I know don't use it in their gardens because it's hard and quite costly to set up. If you live in a dry location that doesn't get much rain in summer, with drip irrigation, you can leave your garden for weeks without worrying about whether your plants are getting enough water. Check out Encyclopedia Botanica's podcast if you want to learn more about drip irrigation in home gardens. If you don't have drip irrigation, the next best thing is to water the plants from the bottom. Set up a watering system and then leave your garden. Overhead irrigation is inefficient because too much water is wasted due to evaporation. You'll have a hefty water bill and potentially unhappy veggie plants as a result. This is because the leaves of squashes, cucumbers, and tomatoes should be kept as dry as possible since they are vulnerable to various fungi and diseases.

- **What time is best for watering?**

Morning is the ideal time to water your garden. Because it is usually colder, less water evaporates throughout the process. Even if your water slides near the plants' base, some water will undoubtedly splash up onto the leaves. Watering in the morning allows the plants' leaves to dry out over the day. Many of us spend our mornings getting ready for work and school, so watering during that time could disorganize our schedules. If this is the case for you, watering in the evening is okay. It's also cold at that time of day, so less water will evaporate. Also, it's much nicer to be out in the garden in the early morning or evening.

- **Mulch your soil.**

Using bare soil to grow a vegetable garden is a bad idea. It encourages the growth of many weeds, and your soil may dry up faster and occasionally break up. On the other hand, thickly mulched gardens need to be watered less often, which means fewer hours of labor for you! In my garden, at the height of summer, I noticed a significant difference in the texture and color of the soil beneath the mulch and the bare soil exposed to the sun and elements. The exposed soil was usually dry and cracking due to a lack of moisture, but the soil behind the mulch was dark, crumbly, chilly, and wet.

Follow these tips to water your vegetables properly:

- Concentrate on the plants' roots—remember that the roots, not the leaves, need water. So, wetting the foliage is a waste of water and might lead to the spread of diseases.
- Water only when necessary—drip irrigation schedules are very useful. Simply keep an eye on the weather and water less often when there is a lot of rain. Note that plants can be harmed by both too much and too little moisture.
- Water deeply—lawns and annuals concentrate their roots in the top 6 inches of soil; perennials, shrubs, and trees concentrate their

roots in the top 12 inches. Water can take several hours to seep through 6-12 inches of thick soil. Check the progress with a finger or a shovel.

- Water in the early hours of the day—this gives the leaves time to dry off if they become wet. Plants hardly get diseases when their foliage is dry.
- Mulch everything—mulch reduces surface runoff and decreases soil evaporation.
- Use the right tool—instead of a sprinkler, use a soaker hose or a more accurate drip irrigation system to irrigate the root zone.

- **Watering a newly planted seed.**

Watering once a week won't provide enough moisture if you are waiting for seeds to germinate. Until germination, keep the top of the soil continuously wet. You should give newly planted garden beds a short bath every 1–2 days, depending on the veggies and the weather. Different veggies take different amounts of time to germinate. For example, spring radishes grow in fewer than seven days, but carrot seeds might take up to three weeks! Both must be constantly watered until the first leaves emerge from the soil. Once the seeds germinate, you may resume your weekly or bi-weekly watering plan, unless the weather is sweltering and dry, in which case they might need more water until they grow.

Gardening requires adequate knowledge about your soil. More than just knowing the type of soil and soil organisms that can keep your soil alive, you must also know how to keep your soil healthy. Soil is much more than just sand and dirt. Soil is a living ecosystem or a vast population of living creatures connected by nutrient cycles and energy fluxes.

So, how can you make your soil healthy?

How to Give More Life to Your Soil

- **Add organic matter.**

Organic matter boosts the basic components of the soil, such as water and air availability, allowing for healthy root development. Organic matter is made up of live plant roots and organisms, decaying plant and animal waste in various stages of decay, and enzymes released by soil organisms that bind soil particles together like glue. Plants gain access to nutrients as soil organisms such as fungi and bacteria break down plant and animal components. The plants' leftovers, in turn, feed the soil microbes. Humus is a highly degraded plant material that is a stable and good source of nutrients for developing plants.

- **Don't starve your soil! Provide enough air and water.**

For optimal growth, plant roots and microorganisms need different amounts of air and water. Fortunately, the soil is rich in microenvironments—tiny ecosystems with varying levels of accessible air, water, and nutrients. Unfortunately, these critical microenvironments can be destroyed by soil compaction and disturbance, such as excessive tillage. As a result, plant roots find it difficult to penetrate the soil, absorb water and nutrients, and interact with helpful microorganisms. Disturbing the soil also disrupts weed seeds, exposing them to light and boosting germination—which means more weeds!

Microbes, organic matter, and soil nutrients abound in the top few inches of soil. Mulch or cover crops can be used to save important topsoil from eroding while also adding rich organic matter as they decay. Raindrops that fall on bare soil can launch soil particles many feet into the air. Mulching topsoil around plants prevents soil particles and pathogens from splashing onto leaves and stems, reducing the risk of disease. By regulating soil temperature, mulch and cover crops preserve soil moisture, decrease weeds, and reduce plant stress.

While most microorganisms are helpful to plants, pathogenic bacteria may survive winter in the soil and plant litter. These organisms prefer to colonize and feed on certain plants. Planting the same crop in the same soil year after year might promote disease development.

- **Practice crop rotation.**

- Crop rotation kills disease-causing bacteria by removing their feeding supply.
- It prevents nutritional deficiency.
- Long-rooted plants, such as carrots, absorb nutrients deeper in the soil.
- Onions with shallow roots receive nutrients in the top few inches of soil.
- Legumes, such as beans and peas, replenish soil nutrients.
- They also form a mutual connection with rhizobia (root-inhabiting bacteria that absorb nitrogen from the air and convert it into a plant-available form to provide nitrogen to the soil).
- When the legumes die, the nitrogen becomes accessible to the rest of the plants in the cycle.

However, before you start the process of crop rotation, take note of these few guidelines:

- Crop rotation is often based on plant families. This is because plants of the same family are usually prone to similar pests and diseases and have similar nutritional and cultural needs.
- Rotate crops from the cabbage family with crops from the sunflower family or the squash family with crops from the grass family.
- Other families, such as carrot and goosefoot, can fill in the gaps in the cycle as needed.
- If you don't have enough planting area to rotate crops, combine several plant families to ensure a diverse crop mix in your vegetable garden.

As I have stated, another vital and noteworthy part of keeping your soil healthy is mulching.

- **Mulching.**

The efficient application of mulch is a defining feature of any healthy garden. Mulches aid in the control of weeds, the prevention of diseases, the conservation of moisture, the regulation of soil temperature, the enrichment of the soil, and the garden's aesthetics. What's more, because of its capacity to reduce foliage and disease, a well-mulched garden can produce more vegetables than a garden that is not mulched enough. However, the effects of mulch are not all positive. So, the type of mulch you choose and the benefits you seek will both be essential considerations. Here are some differences in the types of mulch that you should note:

Organic mulches: Plant resources such as the bark, leaves, needles, grass clippings, or compost are used to make organic mulches. Here are some things to think about while planning your vegetable garden:

Grass clipping: It is better to use dry grass and start building up that layer to a few inches thick. Using a heavy blanket of green grass will cause too much heat and foul odors, instead of decomposing like other organic materials. Grass clippings decompose quickly and supply nitrogen to developing plants. Avoid lawn clippings that have already been treated with pesticides or fertilizers.

Bark and wood chips: Bark and wood chips, one of the most popular forms of mulch, come in various hues and types. As bark and wood chips decompose, the organic matter is pushed into the ground by earthworms and insects that live and burrow in the soil. This improves the soil and promotes healthier plant development. However, bark and wood chips degrade fast. So, they must be replaced regularly to help control weed and retain moisture in your garden.

Compost mulch: The rotting garbage of decomposed organic materials is a desirable resource for gardeners that's mostly made of yard and kitchen waste. Using compost as a mulch will nourish your plants over time. Nitrogen and carbon are fixed into the soil when rain falls on the compost, producing high-quality additions. Compost materials, over time, will renew the soil and remove any pollutants that are stopping your plants from growing well.

You must note some of your garden competitors. They have been around for a long time and will be around even after you stop gardening; don't take them lightly because they don't have a home except among your vegetables. They are **pests and weeds.**

- **Keeping away weeds and pests.**

You can begin your journey toward eco-friendly weed control by following the tips below:

- First, choose fungal-disease-resistant plant types that can be grown in groups, giving weeds less area to thrive.

- Next, design the garden such that there aren't many vacant places for weeds to take over.
- Build layers of plants of varying heights to shade the soil, creating an unpleasant environment for weed seed development.
- Use various ground coverings to hide the exposed soil that many weeds like.
- Plant the vegetable garden in such a way that low-growing plants cover the exposed soil around greater varieties.

- **Cultivating your soil.**

Another option is carefully cultivating your soil. Though over-cultivating your soil can degrade its tilth and texture, using a hoe to cut off small weed seeds shortly after they grow prevents them from maturing. Just be careful not to till or cultivate too thoroughly, or you risk bringing hidden weed seeds to the soil's surface, where they will sprout fast.

- **Topping.**

Even though you don't have the time or energy to root out the entire plant, topping entails clipping off weed blooms and seeds before they shed. This is especially useful for reducing the number of weed seeds in the soil (the weed seed bank). Topping is necessary for dealing with annual weeds like crabgrass, trefoil, lamb's quarters, and purslane, as well as perennial weeds like Canada thistle and dandelions. Trim or weed whack the plants before producing seeds or use a hand scythe to chop off growing seed heads.

- **Companion planting.**

To keep away pests organically, you can try intercropping and companion planting. Companion planting is the method of growing certain plants next to one another to encourage healthy development. In the case of pest management, try companion planting with pest-repellent plants. Garlic is a great choice; growing garlic among your other crops can help reduce the number of pests in your garden. Planting various crops next to one other is known as intercropping. This prevents monocultures, which can serve as a breeding ground for pests. Pests can't infest your garden if they can't locate the proper species to settle on.

- **Look out for pest resistant plants.**

Also, some plants are naturally more pest-resistant than others. Garlic, leeks, and onions are pest-resistant crops. Some root crops, such as radishes, are resistant to insects, though slugs and snails will still eat them. Rhubarb's high amounts of oxalic acid make it naturally pest-resistant. There are also variants of some vegetables developed to resist bugs and other animals that eat them. The King Harry potato, for example, was developed to have hairy leaves that prevent potato bug infestations.

- **Give room for those helping insects.**

Pollinators are essential but don't forget about the other valuable insects in your organic garden. Ladybugs, lacewings, and other helpful insects help keep pests at bay by devouring greenflies and other unwanted bugs. Don't try to introduce them artificially. Instead, grow flowers that will attract beneficial insects. Sunflowers, alyssum, angelica, and other flowers with a flat form and abundant nectar are good examples.

- **Take care of your gardening tools.**

This should be one of your major concerns. Here are ways you can maintain your tools:

- Clean your tools after use—don't ignore their stains.

- Store your tools in a cool and dry area (read the instructions; it's always there).
- Oil your pruning shears.
- Sharpen your tools.
- Clean the wooden handles.

One essential factor for maintaining your garden is pruning. So, by choosing the right plants for your landscape, you can reduce the amount of trimming and plant upkeep you have to handle. But pruning is sometimes necessary. In such situations, using the right timing and method will make the process as easy for you and your plants as possible. Improper trimming can cause a plant to stop flowering, lose its aesthetic value, and even die.

Before you rush off to start cultivating your garden organically, note these 7 commandments:

1. Start your garden—stop procrastinating. You are more than halfway through this book.
2. Get down with good soil—it is for your benefit.
3. Get a good location for your plant; don't assume that every plant needs sun. Some need shade too. *Remember that it's not every time you want to enjoy the cold.*
4. Don't forget the golden rule—water your plants.

5. Prune it; grow it.
6. Don't forget that we are organically structured.
7. Don't be a total cleaner. Instead, leave some fallen fruit to decompose.

KEY TAKEAWAYS

- Maintaining your garden is as important as starting it.
- Consistency will keep you on track and make you a good gardener.
- Have healthy soil, produce beautiful veggies, and clean your garden tools.

---

1. You really don't need to think you have any health-threatening issues because of this; we all feel tired.

7

ADAPTING WITH THE SEASONS

What season of the year do you see as your best? Spring, winter, fall, or summer? You definitely have your reasons for choosing one of these seasons. Perhaps you prefer cold seasons to seasons when you have to wear lighter clothes. Whatever your reasons are, they are valid! As for me, I choose spring. Do you know why? Well, you'll find out later on in this chapter.

In the previous chapter, I walked you through the processes of maintaining your garden, giving it a 5-star layout, and growing the best plants. These tips are what I have learned over the years and what have made me become an excellent organic farmer, which you also long to be. In this chapter, you will learn different ways to grow your garden as the season changes.

Surprised?

Well, don't be. These ways aren't complicated, nor are they hard to achieve. The truth is, even us humans dress differently in every season. We put on a heavy sweater in winter, and prefer lighter clothing in summer. The changes in these seasons also affect the way the plants grow. But how does it affect them? What are the things to take note of? And how can you adapt to each season to have good yields? There are several ways you can care for your garden with each change of the season.

Again, the truth is, you can have a beautiful garden all year. All you need is a solid grasp of what changes each season. You'll need to know how to work with, rather than against, the seasons. When it comes to seasonal growth, it is also vital to consider these changes. This includes thinking about what plants are currently in season and which ones you can plant today for later blooming.

Before I go into the full details of seasoned knowledge, let me quickly give you an overview of gardening seasons.

GARDENING SEASONS

- **Spring**

Welcome to that season when the ground warms up and becomes easier to dig. Spring gardening is refreshing and renewing, as bulbs planted in the fall or early winter begin to bloom. Spring is also a good time to plant perennials and look forward to their bursts of brilliant color as summer approaches.

- **Fall**

Fall is that season that allows gardeners to plan for early spring flowers or vegetables. Mind you, it is also a good time for gardeners to experiment with planting trees and shrubs (if you plan on growing bigger) that will eventually become dormant. Take advantage of the soil in fall before it gets too hard to work on. Act now!

- **Summer**

Annual blooming plants may now take root in milder ground conditions now that frost has passed. As bright sunny flowers emerge, July is no doubt the season that gardeners look forward to all year. You could even arrange for late summer blooms to extend the vibrant display of plants into fall.

- **Winter**

Winter gardening is much more about upkeep and care than it is about planting. This is because the earth becomes moist or complex during winter, making it harder for roots to absorb vital nutrients. So, winter is a great time to focus on maintaining your existing, dormant vegetation so that you can have a much better gardening season in spring.

Now that I have shared the main differences between the four seasons, let's get into the unique gardening problems and planting possibilities that each season offers. If you want the best results, make sure to follow these seasonal growth guides for tips on how to make the most of what each season has to offer.

SEASONAL GARDENING

I promised to give you detailed tips on seasonal gardening. Well, here are they:

Spring Farming

Spring is generally the most rewarding season for both novice and expert gardeners. It's tempting to start planting when the weather warms and frost thaws. But you must first note the sudden changes in growth that spring is known for. Though spring is just one season, it has three mini-seasons, depending on your climate's frost date. You must understand these mini-seasons because they can help you determine which plants are in season now and which must wait until later in spring.

These three mini-seasons are early spring, 3 weeks before frost date, and frost date.

Early spring: This spans the first days of spring. It's important to keep an eye on the soil conditions throughout this period. If the soil is still too hard to work on, it is not yet time to plant. After the earth has softened, you may start planting bare-root perennials and cold-tolerant annuals.

Three weeks before the frost date: The average period when the potential of frost has passed in your area is the frost-free date. Work two to three weeks before this date. This is a great time to plant any flowers that can adapt to your climate. You can now plant potted flowers and outdoor trees and plants. Cold season vegetables, such as leafy greens, can also be grown since they can withstand cold.

After frost date: Once the fear of frost has gone, you may start seeding and transplanting annuals and vegetable plants. This is also an excellent time to dig up and divide perennial plants that haven't flowered yet. Finally, you may start planting summer flowering bulbs now and any non-hardy bulbs or bulb-like plants.

Spring is a delicate season for planting, but it is also a good time to lay out your garden's color palette. Make plans for which flowers and vegetables to grow during the spring planting season. This will help you make the most of your space while also anticipating your garden's seasonal needs.

Tips for Planting in Spring

Prepare your garden beds and soil: After a long winter, the beginning of spring is a great time to prepare your garden beds. First, remove any waste, such as leaves or snow. Next, remove the weeds by pulling them and destroying their roots. Next, take advantage of this time to feed your soil with organic compost and plenty of water. Finally, don't forget to care for any plants that survived winter. To avoid freezing and shock, prune them back after the frost-free date.

Blooming times should be staggered: The key to seasonal gardening is to start planning for flowering seasons in spring. First, choose a location for your early bloomers like cold-tolerant annuals and early-blooming perennials. Before you plant these plants, be sure they've been hardened off at the garden center. Then determine where to put your summer flowering bulbs, which will remain dormant until well into early summer. By anticipating flowering dates, you can guarantee that your garden remains vibrant and beautiful throughout spring and summer.

Plan beauty with gardening: It's time to get creative with your spring gardening. Flowering color palettes may be created based on blooming times. Complementary hues should be grouped together. A warm color palette, for example, might include red, orange, and yellow. Blue and purple are standard colors in cool color schemes. Depending on the size of your beds, you can repeat color combinations to create a unified palette in your garden.

Summer Farming

One thing you should note is that, as you approach the end of spring and the beginning of summer, expect your summer bulbs to begin flowering. You'll also notice that your soil dries up faster, telling you it's time to water deeper into the soil. Because soil conditions change every season, they are essential to improving soil fertility. Also, mulch-rich gardens help the soil retain nutrients, which helps your lovely summer blossoms grow better.

Summer brings its own set of conditions and elements that gardeners must consider while designing seasonal gardens. For example, plants might be stressed when planted or transplanted during hot summer months. According to experts, you shouldn't plant bare-root or recently divided plants since the heat is too dangerous for them. But summer annuals, perennials, and shrubs grown in pots can be planted effectively. These should be heat-tolerant plants that will blossom and flourish all summer long.

Another factor to consider when it comes to summer planting is location. Certain annuals can be scorched by the intense summer heat. So, you must plant them in full or partial shade. But place your sun-loving bloomers where they will get the longest sun exposure.

Although heat is such a concern this time of year, apply the following summer planting tips to ensure a healthy, productive summer garden:

Tips for Planting in Summer

Plant early in summer: Planting might be hard in July and August because of high temperatures. That is why, according to experts, you should plant your summer annuals in June. You may also plant some end-of-summer flowers that will blossom in August during this period. This manner, just the warmest months, will necessitate upkeep and care for your garden. Then, on hot, sunny days, you may sit back and enjoy your garden.

Water thoroughly during planting: Summer heat may quickly dry the soil, making it harder for annual summer plants to flourish. That is why you must properly hydrate your bare soil before planting. Continue to water your annuals as you plant them or move them from pots. Even when you finish planting them, you'll need to maintain the right moisture levels while the roots take hold. Continue to water summer flowers slowly, deeply, and regularly.

Make a soil ditch: You should plan for increased watering needs when planting early summer plants. Annuals have short root systems that quickly dry out the plant. Build a dirt moat around each plant to account for increased watering demands. When watering or when it rains, moats assist in filtering water down towards the roots. This is a simple way to maximize watering efforts and keep your summer crops happy.

You may be able to stretch your late summer garden into October with appropriate care and upkeep. First, remove deadheads as soon as possible. This helps the plants save their energy for maintaining healthy blooms rather than producing seeds. You should also feed your plants throughout summer to ensure that they live as long as possible. Next, remove any dead annuals from your summer beds as you prepare to enter October. This will allow you to make room for your bulbs and any new shrubs or trees. Finally, if you want to pursue container planting during autumn and winter, now is a great time to stock up on containers.

Fall Farming

If you are interested in fall gardening, you must first know your main interest: planting cold-season plants such as shrubs, trees, hardy perennials, and annuals is one priority. Second, you need to prepare for spring flowers by planting autumn bulbs. Keep in mind that you may only have a limited time to do this because you must finish planting before the ground hardens or gets too wet. Neither of these situations is ideal for planting since the soil is either unworkable or has too much moisture for plant roots.

It is essential to prepare your garden for fall before you begin planting. You should pay special attention to any symptoms of illness and pests. If sick plant debris is left in your garden, the diseases might reappear in spring and damage your new-year flowers. Here are some ideas for getting your garden ready for fall and starting your autumn planting:

Clean your soil to allow for nutrient supplements. Dig through your beds and remove all dead plant material, leaves, and weeds. After you've cleaned all of the debris, you may begin to renourish the soil before planting. Nourishing your soil in autumn prepares it for abundant spring growth. To feed microorganisms, use an organic soil amendment and manure. Till the soil well to allow for enough air.

Tips for Planting in Fall

Plant fall bulbs: Planting bulbs that will bloom in spring is best done in fall. This is because the earth is still warm enough for roots to establish themselves before the frost arrives. Bulb roots take six weeks to establish themselves, so work before the predicted frost date. After you've prepared your soil, plant your bulbs in an area that receives partial to full sunlight. Make sure your bulbs are 3–6 inches apart.

Choose vibrant cold-season plants: Just because summer is over doesn't mean your garden's color has to fade. Several cold-season perennials and annuals bloom far into fall to provide a continuous, beautiful autumn. Likewise, filling in landscaping gaps with a blend of perennials, shrubs, and trees that produce bright winter berries is a beautiful idea in fall.

It's now simply a matter of upkeep once you've done your early fall plantings. As we get closer to frost-covered mornings, plants begin to become dormant in preparation for winter. But there is still a lot of activity going on in the soil. Winter gardening is all about encouraging healthy development in spring by engaging in this activity.

Winter Farming

While winter is not the season for planting, it is the season for preparation and care. Winter, like summer, has its own set of gardening conditions and risks to consider. Follow these winter gardening strategies to maintain a healthy winter garden that will still flourish in spring:

Tips for Planting in Winter

Controlling soil temperature: When the earth freezes and hardens, it is important to preserve your soil and plants. This will help your hardy perennials, shrubs, and trees survive winter and avoid freezing temperatures. Uneven ground temperatures are one of the most serious threats to your plants during winter. You can reduce this risk by laying down a thick layer of fresh mulch. This insulates the soil and maintains ground temperatures.

Avoid soil shifting: Another issue to be aware of throughout winter is ground shifting. The constant freezing and thawing might cause the frozen earth to break. It can move your bulbs and force them to the surface if there is enough breaking. Use evergreen boughs as a mulch layer across your bulb beds to prevent soil movement.

Avoid snow heaps: Snow heaps, when used as mulch, can be an excellent soil insulator. But they can also be dangerous to the branches and limbs of delicate trees and plants. The weight of snow, along with the cold weather, might cause limbs to shatter. When you notice snow gathering, make sure to remove it from your plants regularly. Brush snow off branches using a broom or another soft tool. Start at the bottom and work your way up to avoid piling up more snow weight on lower branches.

Plants are dormant throughout winter, but they still need to be watered regularly. Inspect your winter garden regularly for symptoms of damaged limbs and foliage as well as insect infestations. Address any of these problems as soon as possible to offer your plants the best chance of survival. This way, you would have less work to do in spring.

You should know that the brightest gardeners anticipate seasonal changes and even plan for them so that they can take advantage of what each season has to offer. So, here are five ways you can learn how to communicate with your plants and know what they want.

- A competent gardener should constantly learn and adjust to what works and what doesn't.
- Maintain agility and flexibility in your approach and let your plants express their wants and desires to you.
- Preconceived ideas and thoughts that may arise throughout the dialogue with your plants should be avoided. Instead, allow things to happen naturally.

- Socialize with the plants and provide them with existential nature.
- Focus when communicating with your plants. Even though you have a lot of ideas rushing through your head right now, try to find some stillness.

Do you ever notice any changes in flavor or prices when you buy fruits and vegetables? The truth is, there are several reasons for this, but the most important reason is the season they were grown in. Some fruits and vegetables grow better in summer or spring and cost more during winter because they are harder to grow. So, it's essential to know the peak seasons for each variety of fruit and vegetable before deciding when to buy them.

SOME SEASONAL CROPS YOU SHOULD KNOW

Winter	Spring	Summer	Fall
Oranges	Mustard greens	Blackberries	Swiss chard
Leeks	Fennel	Broccoli	Garlic
Rutabaga	Celeriac	Zucchini	Cauliflower
Turnips	Asparagus	Watermelon	Mushrooms
Grapefruits	Collards	Green beans	Potatoes
Chestnuts	Carrots	Tomatoes	Pumpkin
Lemon	Chives	Plums	Sweet potatoes
Kale	Artichoke	Raspberries	Ginger
Tangerines	Rhubarb	Cucumber	Pomegranate
Radishes	Apricots	Blueberries	Figs
-	Fava beans	Peaches	Pears
-	Strawberries	-	Apples
-	Morsels	-	Cranberries

Likewise, below is a list of vegetables that best work with all seasons.

Vegetables available all year round:

- Celeriac (Celery root)
- Bok choy
- Broccoflower
- Broccolini
- Burdock root
- Celery
- Cherry tomatoes
- Black-eyed peas
- Black radish
- Cabbage
- Carrots
- Chinese eggplants
- Galangal root
- Onions
- Parsnips
- Pearl onions
- Potatoes
- Rutabagas
- Amaranth
- Arrowroot
- Banana squash
- Bell peppers
- Leek
- Lettuce
- Mushrooms

- Olives

Vegetables available in spring:

- Mustard greens
- Pea pods
- Peas
- Purple asparagus
- Radicchio
- Ramps
- Artichokes
- Asparagus
- Belgian endive
- Red leaf lettuce
- Rhubarb
- Snow peas
- Morel mushrooms
- Sorrel
- Spinach
- Spring baby lettuce
- Butter lettuce
- Cactus
- Fiddlehead ferns
- Manoa lettuce
- Chayote squash
- Corn

Vegetables available in fall:

- Butter lettuce
- Buttercup squash
- Belgian endive
- Black salsify
- Broccoli
- Delicata squash
- Daikon Radish
- Endive
- Swiss chard
- Turnips
- Brussels sprouts
- Butternut squash
- Garlic
- Ginger
- Jalapeno peppers
- Jerusalem artichoke
- Kohlrabi
- Pumpkin
- Radicchio
- Sweet dumpling squash
- Acorn squash
- Sweet potatoes
- Cauliflower
- Chayote squash
- Chinese long beans

Vegetables available in winter:

- Leeks
- Sweet dumpling squash
- Sweet potatoes
- Turnips
- Winter squash
- Belgian endive
- Brussels sprouts
- Buttercup squash
- Collard greens
- Delicata squash
- Kale

Vegetables available in summer:

- Radishes
- Shallots
- Sugar snap peas
- Summer squash
- Tomatillo
- Tomatoes
- Winged beans
- Butter lettuce
- Chayote squash
- Chinese long beans
- Corn

- Crookneck squash
- Cucumbers
- Eggplant
- Endive
- Garlic
- Green beans
- Green soybeans (edamame)
- Jalapeno peppers
- Lima beans
- Yukon gold potatoes
- Zucchini
- Beets
- Bell peppers
- Manoa lettuce
- Okra
- Peas

As a good gardener, you must know how to protect your plant throughout these different seasons to keep your efforts intact. Surely, you don't want all your efforts wasted! This is why I have provided ways you can take to avoid that below.

DAMAGE CONTROL: SIDE-STEPPING HAZARDOUS SEASONS

Winter

- **Add a mulch layer.**

After the first severe freeze, apply a 3- to 5-inch layer of mulch. You don't have to buy wood mulch. Because they are not compact, lightweight materials such as chopped leaves and pine straw are great options. Mulch is a garden wonder worker at any time of year and is an essential component of winter maintenance. Think of mulch as a covering that protects the garden during cold months. Soil heave or elevation caused by freeze-thaw cycles is a typical winter issue. Adding mulch helps to keep the soil wet and offers insulation for plants that are only slightly hardy.

- **Water in winter.**

Watering gardens in winter may seem pointless since many plants are dormant. Still, there are solid reasons to irrigate throughout winter months. Evergreen trees and shrubs lose a lot of water in cold, dry weather, especially on windy days. These plants need extra watering (at least once every month) to keep the soil wet throughout the winter season unless you get enough rainfall. Additionally, winter irrigation is beneficial to even dormant plants. Even while the canopy is dormant, many plants still develop roots actively.

- **Guard those little sensitive trees.**

Trees with weak or smooth bark may gain from a stem wrap in late fall to shield the trunk from a condition known as southwest damage or sunscald. This damage is caused by the freezing and thawing of water in the trunk and occurs in the southwest section of the trunk, which is exposed to the warm afternoon sun. Wrap young, thin-barked trees in a commercial protective material to avoid winter sunscald. It is important to remove trunk covers in spring to avoid damage. Newly planted trees may also need stability, but not all trees need to be stalked. Shake the tree slightly from side to side to see if staking is required. The tree's base should stay stable in the ground. If you can see the root ball moving, it's time to stake the tree for winter.

- **Store your water features away from freezing and breaking.**

To safeguard your investment during winter, most modest water features require some winter preparation. The first tip is to keep the pump from freezing. Remove the pump and keep it indoors during winter in places where it won't freeze. Ceramic vases can break when exposed to cold temperatures. You should drain water from ceramic features and bring them indoors during winter in chilly climates. Remember to bring any tropical plant materials, including tropical water lilies, indoors for winter in water gardens. Check with your local garden pond experts to see whether your pump can keep pumping water throughout the year or if it has to be removed and stored till winter.

Just as you give your house a thorough spring cleaning to help freshen it up after a long winter, you can do the same for your yard to prepare it for the warmer months. Even after the snow and ice have melted, handling all of the labor needed for a picture-perfect spring landscape can be daunting. Use this checklist to help you stay on track while you clean up your flower beds, trees, and bushes, as well as other parts of your yard.

Spring

- **Clean the flower beds.**

Clear any dead leaves or other debris from winter storms from the soil surface where you plan to grow annual flowers and vegetables. Cut down last year's withered leaves and remove protective winter mulch from around perennials and decorative grasses.

- **Divide the perennials first.**

Many perennials gain from being divided shortly before their spring growth begins. Dividing perennials is a cheap way to add extra plants to your yard or share them with friends. It's also great for maintaining the health of your current perennials. If your plants grow in a huge clump, their center might thin out after a few years, creating a barren patch.

- **Plant your vegetables.**

Potatoes, artichokes, peas, and certain lettuces sprout best in cold soil, so plant them in early spring after the earth has thawed. By early June, they should be ready for harvest.

Fall

A little fall planning and preparation can get the spring season going. Fall is a great time to clean up beds, control soils, prepare sod, and avoid issues in the upcoming growing season. It's also a good time to plant spring-flowering bulbs and remove fragile summer bloomers. Fall garden preparation is one of those maintenance tasks that will ensure a beautiful and productive garden the following season. Follow these fall garden recommendations for a stress-free winter and more free time in spring:

- **Clear old plants.**

It is time to remove your wasted vegetable plants, tidy up plant debris and weeds, and winterize your lawn furniture and water features towards the end of the season. Raking leaves onto the lawn and mowing them with a grass catcher are two simple fall landscaping ideas. This is also a good opportunity to get rid of invasive plants.

- **Get your garden to bed.**

Dig up any delicate bulbs or tubers and bring them in. Take your plants indoors if there is a prolonged cold. Removing plant waste and raking will help to reduce the number of insects, diseases, and weed seeds that might show up over winter. Empty the compost containers and begin over. Spread the compost around the base of vulnerable plants that might benefit from the extra layer as a blanket. In your vegetable garden, plant a cover crop.

Summer

Gardening in the heat can be hard. But here are some practical tips for getting the most out of your indoor and outdoor plants in summer:

- **Try pot planting.**

Container gardening is becoming popular in outdoor design. Container gardening is generally the only choice for renters with balconies. Homeowners may use brightly colored planters and pots to complement flower gardens and lawns. But keep in mind that containers need maintenance too.

- **Add compost made from leftover food.**

Remember the ways of making organic compost in chapter 4? Apply it here. Plants, like all living things, need food. Nutrient-dense soil not only supplies most of your plants' essential nutrients but also provides a healthy boost to your soil garden. Use leftover cooked veggies on your potted patio plants. Not only will this assist in watering your plants and preserving fresh resources, but the remaining vitamins and minerals from your cooked vegetables will help your garden thrive.

- **Give space for your garden plants.**

Potted plants are visually appealing and add vertical dimension to landscapes, but many blooms need ground room to grow well. If you don't have enough yard space to grow flowers in the ground, choose patio containers instead.

- **Pests! Beware.**

Use a spray bottle filled with a natural blend of lemon juice and water to repel pests like snails, slugs, and aphids. Lemons' nutrients also give extra health benefits to your new plants. Don't overlook larger animals such as squirrels and birds. Distract little animals by placing feeders far away from the garden. If you have cats, cover flowers with pine straw and sprinkle ground cinnamon on top to discourage their attention.

- **Water wisely.**

Watering plants using a standard garden hose is the least effective method. Consider investing in a soaker hose or sprinkler nozzle for more efficient watering. Perennials only need 1–2 inches of water every week—any more can be harmful. Watering should be limited to the root zone of your plants, which is the few inches surrounding a plant's canopy. Water plants in the morning when temperatures are low, giving them enough time to absorb the water before the heat evaporates it.

KEY TAKEAWAYS

- Plants have feelings too,[1] and only you can help them live through different seasons.
- The responsibility of having a good garden lies in your hands.[2]
- Follow the processes wisely.

---

1. Interpret that anyhow you like.
2. Palms, actually.

8

HARVEST LIKE A BOSS

Were you wondering if harvesting also has its own techniques? Oh yes! Would you like to harvest what will not give you the satisfaction of all your labors throughout the past seven chapters? Trust me—there are expert ways to harvest your crops. In fact, there are ways to know if a crop is ready for harvest. So, in this chapter, I am going to give you a breakdown of harvesting like a boss. This includes mistakes to avoid during harvest, signs to watch out for, ways to handle your vegetables, and my tips to help you achieve your dream of becoming a gardener. So, are you ready to learn?

Harvest is that period filled with joy and pride of seeing all your labor from the day you started out till the day you figured your crops are ready. It is a period that every farmer looks forward to, when your soul is refreshed from all the workdays. It is also your reward for the tillings and organic farming methods you followed. So, basically, harvest is when every farmer gets the best from what they have once buried.

Harvesting takes different approaches, and one of these approaches is knowing the mistakes to avoid in harvesting. To be able to understand this better, I have gone the extra mile in discussing these for you.

AVOID THESE HARVESTING MISTAKES

Never assume that your plants will just come out as planned. Sometimes, the soil, weather, and every other factor determining your harvest might not work as planned, which is why you should never skip this section. So, back to our discussion, what mistakes should you watch out for as a beginner in farming? Here they are:

- **Harvesting your vegetables late.**

Sometimes, the patient dog gets to eat a shrunken bone. And this can be the same story when it comes to harvesting. So, harvest quickly, but never too quickly. Different vegetables have different timelines and harvests. The issue is that sometimes you can get so caught up in admiring your work that you forget it's time to harvest. As a result, you might get overripe vegetables that are moldy, rotten, and only fit for the trash can. If you garden in a cold environment, you may end up with frost-damaged vegetables that will never make it to the veggie soup pot. Also, failing to harvest at the right time leads to overburdened branches and stalks, which can greatly reduce your garden's output.

- **Harvesting incorrectly.**

Did you know that vegetables can still continue to ripen even after they've been picked? You've most likely seen this before. As an organic gardener, you can increase the probability of ripening your vegetables well by being extra careful when removing them from the garden. Find out what time of day is best for picking the vegetables you're ready to harvest. Crops like peas and sweet corn, for example, should be picked early in the morning (or right before you plan to eat them) and kept cool to ensure the best taste and quality. And remember to be gentle when harvesting your vegetable garden! Picking delicate vegetables, like cucumbers and tomatoes, should be done with care to avoid bruises and split skin, which can lead to soft, mushy parts.

- **Washing vegetables incorrectly before storing.**

If you're a neat freak, the dirt may not make you happy when you're harvesting carrots in your vegetable garden. And, if these are going to be part of today's meal, wash them now. Do you plan on storing these beautiful vegetables that you've worked so hard to grow? Then, never forget to wash them first.

- **Not storing harvested vegetables very well.**

Storing your harvested vegetables the right way can greatly improve their quality. But I have learned over the years that many novice gardeners don't know how much exposure to light, moisture, inadequate ventilation, and the wrong storage conditions can hurt their first harvest. When there is too much moisture in the storage area, the harvest rots and molds quickly. Poor ventilation causes wilting and tissue collapse in leafy vegetables as well as more fibrous vegetables. Also, the wrong temperatures could make your veggies rotten or —in the case of onions, garlic, potatoes, and carrots— cause extra sprouting, which isn't what you want if you plan to eat them rather than save them for next year's garden. Canning your vegetables is one of the best ways to store them for a long time.

- **Missing on succession planting.**

Not every vegetable is planted and harvested only once a year. Some of them can be harvested many times, allowing you to enjoy the bounty of your garden for months. Depending on the location, vegetables like lettuce, chives, and radishes can produce many crops in a single growing season if you use succession planting. Succession planting involves growing new seeds every few weeks to allow for the growth of new crops. Check out the suggestions for your growing area. Just don't let all the time and effort you put into planning and planting your first vegetable garden go to waste. Harvest each crop properly to maximize freshness and quality so that you and your family can reap the rewards of your labor!

Isn't it exciting to see your first vegetable garden shoots spring up from the soil? It's also fun to watch your first garden grow over the summer. When I was growing up, my younger brother would plant something, and he would keep going back to it every day. And the day the good plant (mainly maize and beans) decided to sprout, I saw him jumping around, feeling accomplished. And the truth is, we are all like that. But learning these mistakes and, more importantly, avoiding them is a great way for us to deal with harvest heartbreak.[1]

In addition to all these, there are also some things you should keep in mind during harvesting. Never forget the reason for all these: you want to harvest like the boss you are!

HARVEST PERIOD: THINGS TO KEEP IN MIND

You put in a lot of effort to finally harvest, but how do you know when it's time to pick? This is a frequently asked question among gardeners. We have this misconception that what we grow in our backyards will look exactly like what we find on a grocery store shelf. But there are a few things you should always keep in mind during the harvest season or as it draws closer.

- **Never forsake your garden—check daily.**

It will hit you all at once when your garden begins to ripen. It's just how the cookie crumbles. So, it is important to inspect your garden on a daily basis. If you don't do this, you may not only miss out on your produce, but you may also allow the produce to rot in your garden. This attracts pests, which means your garden could be infected with a disease in no time. None of this is good, which is why you should inspect your garden on a daily basis. This way, you get the harvest you worked so hard for, and it will continue like this because there will be nothing to attract bugs. Also, remember that picking your plants when they are first ripe usually encourages the plants to produce more.

- **Never underestimate the little things—pick small.**

Have you ever gone to pick zucchini, only to discover that it is the size of a football? Well, that's not good. Don't wait until your vegetables have grown too large. When picking produce, it is best to pick it when it is small. Most vegetable varieties are at their tenderest, have the best flavor, and haven't developed too many seeds at this point. But if you happen to come across a football-sized zucchini, don't toss it. Instead, grate it and use it to make sweet chocolate zucchini bread. When it comes to zucchini, it is best to pick them when they are about 6 inches long. It may not seem like much, but if your plant is running at full capacity (as it usually is), you'll have plenty to go around.

- **Be gentle with the plant.**

Harvesting is a great task, especially when you assign it to your children. It's also fun for your children to be able to pick things from plants. If you need your children to help out, make sure to remind them to be gentle with the produce. Vegetables are prone to being bruised. So it's important to pick them up gently and place them in a basket or bucket. It's not just a question of appearance. If you bruise the skin of the produce, it might rot, reducing the lifespan of the vegetable once harvested. If this happens, you must cook it right away or it will go bad. Even so, it is better to avoid this scenario altogether than to have to cook your harvest in order not to lose it.

- **Lookout—watch where you step!**

When harvesting your vegetables, you must be careful of where you step. Gardens can be hard to navigate. So, you'll need to either have clear walkways or be careful where you put your feet. Else you might step on vegetables that need to be harvested without realizing it or step on other plants. This could harm the plants and open the door for diseases and pests to infiltrate and harm them, making your harvest suffer. It's amazing how something as simple as watching where you walk can help your garden and harvest.

- **Keep track; don't lose your focus.**

The truth is, when you grow an entire garden, it can be hard to keep track of what you planted, what diverse range you have, how long it takes to reach harvest, and what the plants should look like once they're ready for harvest. You'll need to keep track of the data as you go through harvest. You'll know when to begin looking for harvest from each plant if you know which variety you planted and how long it takes it to reach harvest. Also, by knowing which variety you planted, you will have a better idea of what the harvest should look like, which will help you avoid harvesting mistakes.

- **Check for any diseases in your ready-to-harvest plants.**

When you're harvesting, it's a good time to check on the health of your plants. First, you should inspect the leaves for any spots or discoloration. These could be symptoms of a disease or pest invading your garden. If you find that you rarely have time to check on your plants, make it a habit to do so every day when you are out picking. Nothing will escape your notice, and the health of your plants will not suffer. It's another easy step, but it could save your harvest.

- **Be hopeful, but don't be unrealistic.**

When you grow your own vegetables, you'll notice that they don't always look like the ones you buy at the store. For example, the broccoli you grow might not sprout heads as large as the ones in grocery stores. Unrealistic expectations can cause problems during harvest. The next thing you know, you're waiting for them to look like what you're used to seeing, and they end up rotting before you can even harvest them. That said, it's important to understand what your harvest should look like. This way, you'll be prepared and won't miss out on a perfect harvest since your garden simply can't meet your expectations.

- **Let the fruits hang.**

Plants such as tomatoes, apple trees, peppers, and peaches are all products of a plant. You shouldn't pluck these too early. Instead, allow them to ripen on the plant fully. Always remember this when harvesting your garden. This way, you won't over pick certain types of vegetation.

- **Even though rain is good, avoid it sometimes.**

Vegetable gardeners understand how important it is for plants to receive consistent moisture. Still, it's a good idea to stay out of the garden when it is raining. This is especially true for disease-prone crops such as tomatoes, cucumbers, squash, and beans. Additionally, avoid harvesting or working around these vegetables in wet weather. Harvesting can be hard at times, with constant rain and humidity hindering our efforts. Every few days, it might seem like there are more showers, and every night might be wet and humid. This can cause yield loss, soggy fields, quantity loss, and sometimes costly field cleanup (if your farm is big).

- **Harvest often, but only at the right time.**

Even before we pick them, all fruits and vegetables have ways of telling us when they are at their best. But recognizing these signs takes practice. Even the most experienced gardeners may try several times before they can capture that fleeting moment when a not-quite-ripe melon tastes bland and an overripe melon tastes bad. Many factors influence the flavor of your vegetables, including seed variety, soil type, temperature, season, water, sunlight, and whether they are grown in the ground or in a greenhouse. But the most important factors to consider when it comes to harvesting are the time of day and ripeness. If you can't fit a morning harvest into your schedule or lifestyle, pick an evening harvest, but after the heat of the late afternoon sun has begun to fade. Other fruiting vegetables, such as tomatoes, peppers, and zucchini, are less prone to wilting and can be harvested later in the day.

Root vegetables, such as carrots, can also be stored in the refrigerator, but remove them from the sun as soon as possible, especially if the weather is warm. From tapping and smelling melons to puncturing corn kernels and recognizing the perfect plumpness, testing for ripeness involves all of your senses!

- **Use the best harvesting tools.**

Many vegetables, such as beans, peas, lettuce, and kale, do not need harvesting tools. But for crops like zucchini, large-fruited tomatoes, potatoes, cucumbers, and carrots, it is necessary to use a sharp knife, pruning shears, garden fork, or other tools to avoid damaging the plant or the part being harvested. Damaged plants allow diseases, and fruits like zucchini and tomatoes bruise easily, reducing storage and eating quality. To prevent damage and allow for easy washing, place harvested vegetables in a basket, trug, heavy-duty garden cart, or handy garden colander.

Having learned all the things you need to know about the harvesting period, it is also important that you keep in mind the ways to preserve and care for your vegetables and fruits.

WHEN TO HARVEST

What you may not know is that, even before you select the plants, all fruits and vegetables have methods of alerting us when they are at their finest. Would you also like to know the right time to harvest your vegetables and plants? Here are some ways you can know that your plants are ready to harvest.

Don't forget, do it as stated to get the best result.

- **Lettuce**

Pick lettuce early in the morning when the leaves are still crisp. Lettuce comes in two varieties: delicate baby greens and crisp, full-bodied heads. To harvest using the "Cut and Come Again" method, cut lettuce with scissors when they reach approximately 4-5 inches tall and about 2 inches above the soil line. Water well and mildly fertilize to reap several more cuttings. Harvest entire heads of lettuce when they begin to fill in at the center but before they lengthen and "bolt" (send up a flower stalk), at which point they will taste bitter.

- **Tomatoes**

Pick tomatoes when they are vividly colored and have no sign of green on the skin for the finest sun-ripened flavor. If you have alternatively rainy and dry weather and are concerned about cracking of thin-skinned heirlooms, harvest them when they are just tinged with color and let them ripen indoors (not in the refrigerator). Tomatoes taste best when the days and nights are warm; otherwise, even the most excellent kinds might taste tasteless when the evenings are chilly or the sun refuses to shine! Ripe tomatoes should not be stored in the refrigerator for the greatest flavor and texture.

- **Spinach**

Cut young spinach when it is approximately 5-6 tall above the soil line using the "Cut and Come Again" method, and plants will regenerate for another cutting. Alternatively, you may begin picking outer leaves as soon as the plants have at least 5-6 full-size leaves, always keeping at least four to five leaves on the plant to allow it to regenerate easily. By harvesting often with one of these ways, you can lengthen the time it takes for the plant to develop leaves before sending up a flower stalk and "bolting".

- **Pepper**

Sweet peppers smell sweeter and are more nutritious when allowed to fully color upon the vine, from green to blazing red, orange, or yellow, depending on the type. If your growing season is too short to allow peppers to fully mature, harvest your final green peppers as late as possible and store them in a cool location to color up, inspecting them frequently for rotting. Chili peppers achieve their maximum pungency and fruitiness when completely colored, although they can be plucked bright green as soon as they reach maturity.

- **Fennel**

When the bulbing fennel base gets knobby and rounded, about 3/4 the size of a tennis ball or larger, cut it at soil level. Cut the ferny leaves down to the stem after collecting each bulb, then slice up the juicy bulb to use fresh or cooked.

- **Eggplant**

Pick eggplants after they have reached their full size and are smooth and glossy. When they are young, before the skins toughen and the seeds grow and brown within, they taste the most delicate and least bitter. To prevent harming the easily broken plants, clip the fruits off the branches rather than pulling the eggplants off.

- **Broccoli**

Broccoli should be harvested in the morning, when the heads are big and completely grown. The buds should grow firmly closed; they will ultimately develop and bloom into golden blossoms. But if you wait too long, your broccoli will be harsh and woody. To stimulate the formation of side branches, cut the plant approximately midway down the stalk. Plants should be kept adequately hydrated to avoid acquiring a harsh or sulfuric flavor. Broccoli tastes best when grown in cold temperatures.

- **Kale**

When the plants are strong and well-established, you may begin harvesting the outer leaves of kale. After harvest, leave seven or eight leaf crowns to regenerate.

- **Onions**

When young onions are 10-12 inches tall, pick them. Wait until about half of the tops have died back and fallen over before harvesting huge storage onions. Knock down the remaining tops and leave them in the ground for another week. Harvest and store in a cold, dry, and airy location. When the skin and tips are totally dry, cut off the tops and shorten the roots.

- **Melons**

Melon beauty is so short that obtaining a perfectly ripe melon every time is an art form. When picking, pay great attention so you may understand what variables suggest the best fruits. If you're having difficulties producing excellent melons in your region, it's possible that your environment is too cold. Grow them on black plastic or over a rock wall, and try several types to discover the best ones for your area.

- **Pumpkins**

Harvest pumpkins once the fruits are deep orange and the shells are so strong that a finger cannot be pierced through them. Slice a 2-3 stem handle, cure in the sun or a warm, dry chamber for 10 days (do not expose to frost), and keep in a cold, dry location at about 50 degrees.

HANDLE YOUR VEGGIES WITH LOVE AND CARE

Fruits and vegetables are the most thrown away foods. Everyone has had to throw away some of their produce at some point, whether it was bananas that went bad or tomatoes that went soft. But you can keep your veggies out of the garbage! Here are ways to help you care for your fruits and vegetables:

- **Keep bananas in a separate place.**

Ripe bananas release a lot of ethylene, which causes all the fruits and vegetables to ripen quickly. So, store bananas at room temperature. Also, it would be best if you separate the bananas from the bunch and wrap their tops in a cling film to slow the ripening process. This prevents bananas from ripening at the same time and reduces the amount of ethylene released.

- **Keep watermelons away from apples.**

Similarly, apples have a high ethylene content, which can be especially harmful to fruits like watermelons and cucumbers. Ethylene can cause them to lose their texture and become mushy much faster than usual.

- **Wash properly.**

Greens with thick leaves prefer humidity but not wetness because it makes them turn yellow. After washing, make sure to thoroughly dry salad greens such as iceberg lettuce, romaine lettuce, and rocket. Wrap them in a dry towel (yes, a regular face towel!) and place them in the fridge. Also, wash delicate herbs like mint, coriander, and basil before using them. Keep them in the fridge in a glass with a small amount of water, just like flowers.

- **Store in a cool and dry place.**

As with most edibles, this also applies to some of the vegetables and fruits which you will harvest. If you have a cellar, store onions and potatoes there. Otherwise, store them in a shaded corner of your kitchen, but be careful not to pile them up, as onions can make potatoes go bad. Remove the tops of root vegetables before storing them. This will keep them moist and preserve their texture and flavor.

Keep a bowl of bright yellow lemons on the counter, though lemons will last only one week if stored this way. But they will last four weeks if stored in the refrigerator. Cucumbers and aubergines dislike cold. So, if you're going to eat them in a few days, leave them out on the counter. Mushrooms should be wrapped in brown paper and stored in the fruit and vegetable drawer. Air can circulate through the paper, and the drawer will keep the air moist.

Instead of putting tomatoes in the fridge, leave them at room temperature on the counter to continue ripening. Line them up side by side, stem side down, in a basket that allows air to circulate. Refrigerating them prevents ripening, inhibits flavor development, and makes the flesh granular. Carrots are best stored in the refrigerator wrapped in a paper towel. If you have enough space, you can store them in a container filled with water. If the carrots still have their tops on them, cut them off and save them separately.

- **Don't store fruits and vegetables together.**

Fruits and vegetables need different amounts of moisture to stay fresh. Fruits need a drier climate than vegetables. Also, because fruits produce more ethylene than vegetables, it is best to keep them in separate compartments of your refrigerator.

Storing your harvest is an excellent way to deal with surpluses and months when there is little growing. Vegetables can be preserved in various ways, including drying and freezing. Plus, there are effective ways to preserve any extra crop, ensuring that you reap the benefits of all your hard work without allowing things to spoil or end up in the compost unnecessarily.

- **Store and preserve your garden harvest.**

Some fruits and vegetables can be stored for months if stored properly. The key to success is to select fresh specimens and inspect them regularly, removing any diseased items. One rotten apple, for example, can ruin the entire batch. On the other hand, crops will not rot if stored in a dry, well-ventilated area. You can buy storage boxes, but a wooden crate or shallow cardboard box will do too. Some boxes and crates are designed to be stacked, but make sure that air can circulate between the levels if you decide to use them.

- **Infusing with alcohol.**

Preservation is as simple as ABC - well, at least when it comes to preserving with alcohol. Fill a sterilized canning jar halfway with washed fruits, then top it off with brandy, vodka, or another high-proof alcohol, preferably the one you prefer. To sweeten things up, add some sugar, close the top, and shake. Now you can enjoy your "drunken" fruit. That is all there is to it.

- **The fermentation method.**

This is an age old method of preservation. If you have abundant cucumbers or cabbage, and you are already thinking of disposing of them - don't! Try the fermenting method. Put your cucumber and spice into a salt-water solution, then store in a cold environment for a few weeks, which will result in the development of lactic acid, and that is your preservative method. Layer shredded cabbage with salt, place it into a pickling jar, cover it with brine, and let it ferment for three to six weeks. You'll have tangy pickles and sauerkraut to jar and process in a water-bath canner at the end of the process. Bonus point: fermented foods are high in probiotics, and they are best for your belly.

- **Canning your foods.**

Canning is as simple as following a recipe - but do you follow a recipe? The results capture sun-ripened flavors in ways that complement family dinners best. The most unique thing about canned food is that home-canned foods saves money on groceries while also providing preservative-free food. Despite the lack of artificial preservatives, home-canned goods are safe to eat for years, albeit quality deteriorates over time. Most canned vegetables, meats, and soups taste best when consumed within a year or two of opening.

- **Freezing your harvest.**

Freezing your harvest is a quick and easy way to preserve it. Freeze the produce in manageable quantities so that it can be easily defrosted. However, you can use only firm, freshly harvested fruits and vegetables and freeze them as soon as possible after harvesting. Place them in an airtight freezer bag or plastic container to ensure they last and don't get "freezer burn" (inedible dry, brown patches caused by lack of moisture). Before freezing, some fruits and vegetables will need to be blanched. Blanching keeps the water in the fruits and vegetables from crystallizing and rupturing the plants' cell walls, resulting in a soggy, soft texture when defrosted.

- **Drying your harvest.**

Tomatoes, peppers, and apples are examples of crops that dry well. Drying can significantly alter the flavor and texture of your crop, making for interesting additions to dishes. Simply wash and thinly slice your fruit or vegetables before placing them in a single layer on a baking sheet. Traditionally, this can be left outside to dry out during long, sunny days. When the pieces are dry, store them in a sterile, airtight container and eat them within a few weeks.

Storing your harvest gives you the peace of mind to have enough without the fear of them ending up in the trash can. You have toiled to produce this bountiful harvest. Now is the time to enjoy your labor, my friend.

KEY TAKEAWAYS

- Knowing how to harvest will save you the heartbreak of losing your vegetables and fruits during harvest.
- Use the best tools for harvesting.
- Storing your harvest gives your soul enough rest and the joy of having enough.
- Organic farming is a lifelong journey.

Don't stop being organic! For your health, for your pocket, and for Mother Earth.

---

1. Harvesting can really be a heartbreaker when the expectations are not met.

CONCLUSION

Going through the journey of being an organic gardener may look unachievable, but trust me, it is 100 percent possible. All it takes is preparing and reading this book.

This book discusses how to be an organic farmer through chapters, boycotting all the inorganic fruits and vegetables you eat and embracing them as given by nature. You don't have to stress yourself on any topics that may be racing through your head at the moment about organic farming because I have discussed it all with you in a humorous way—and also, I've made it simple for you when you start.

I've brought my knowledge of organic gardening from when I was old enough to know what leaves are into this book to improve your understanding of what organic farming is and how you can do it yourself.

You might be wondering why you should grow your food when you can just order some. Well, there are lots of advantages. I mean, think about your purse (you won't be spending much when you can pick them from your backyard and store them). Think about having a good sight of green vegetables and the refreshing pastimes in your garden.

The truth is, everything you need to prepare is what you see every day, but don't take note of because you have not been ready to go organic. For example, you see your soil but do you know what type of soil it is? Likewise, going organic gives you different gardening methods. Using any of these methods will bring optimal success to your farm produce.

But what about fertilizers? How can you farm without adding fertilizer? Of course, you are adding fertilizer and the fun part is that you are making it yourself. The essence of it all is to be organic to the core. This book goes deeper into organic farming, including tips on how you can make your own fertilizer.

And, of course, you have a list of the best veggies and fruits that will bloom in your garden as well as ways to maintain your garden and the veggies, including how you can keep the bugs, pests and weeds away—all organically.

And, finally, making the best of it all—your toil and maintenance. Nothing satisfies the soul more than looking at your harvest in a basket.

Now, what next?

You have all the information at your grasp now. Take a seat and begin drawing out your plans. You don't have any reason to procrastinate. Instead, bring those booming thoughts to action.

Would you like to let me know how this book has helped you? You can drop a review with either a cute smile or a straight face. Don't worry, I am all ears.

A SPECIAL GIFT TO OUR READERS

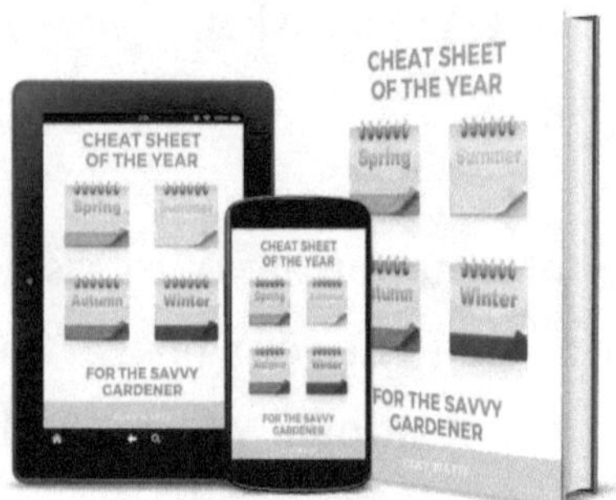

Included with your purchase of this book is our Cheat Sheet of the Year for The Savvy Gardener. In this cheat sheet, you'll have a list of a few tricks, tips, and reminders to do every month of the year to start or maintain your garden.

Scan the QR code below and let us know what email address to deliver it to.

RESOURCES

Gardening to Reduce Your Carbon Footprint! (2015, May 20). Terrapass. https://terrapass.com/blog/gardening-reduce-carbon-footprint

Godman, H. (2012, June 29). *Backyard gardening: grow your own food, improve your health.* Harvard Health Publishing. https://www.health.harvard.edu/blog/backyard-gardening-grow-your-own-food-improve-your-health-201206294984

Gorenje Life SImplified. (2018, March 21). *Why home-grown fruit and vegetables are the best.* https://international.gorenje.com/life-simplified/home-simplified/why-homegrown-fruit-and-vegetables-are-the-best

Iowa State University & Haynes, C. (n.d.). *Can a Vegetable Garden Save You Money?* https://www.extension.iastate.edu/news/2009/mar/060201.htm

Johnson, M. (2010, July 30). *Health Benefits of Home-Grown Produce.* U.S.News. https://health.usnews.com/health-news/diet-fitness/cancer/articles/2010/07/30/health-benefits-of-home-grown-produce

National Geographic & CERNANSKY, R. (2018, November 20). *We don't have enough organic farms. Why not?* https://www.nationalgeographic.com/environment/article/organic-farming-crops-consumers

Nick, J. (2016, December 30). *The History of how organic farming was lost.* NaturesPath. https://www.naturespath.com/en-us/blog/the-history-of-how-organic-farming-was-lost/

Triangle Pest Control. (2017, April 27). *What Are the Environmental Benefits of Growing Your Own Food?* https://www.trianglepest.com/blog/what-are-environmental-benefits-growing-your-own-food

United Nations. (n.d.). *The World's Food Supply is Made Insecure by Climate Change.* https://www.un.org/en/academic-impact/worlds-food-supply-made-insecure-climate-change

Wholesome Hub & Abram, S. (2019, August 07). *The 8 Benefits of Growing Your Own Food.* https://www.wholesomehub.net.au/blog/the-8-benefits-of-growing-your-own-food/

CaliKim29 Garden & Home DIY. (2018, March 11). *How to Prepare Your Garden Soil for Planting Vegetables in 3 Easy Steps // Spring Garden Series #8.* Youtube. https://www.youtube.com/c/CaliKim29/about

EatingWell & Reilly, K. (2020, April 15). *The Only Tools You Need to Start a Garden.* https://www.eatingwell.com/article/17068/the-only-tools-you-need-to-start-a-garden/

Modern Farmer & Barth, B. (2016, February 29). *10 Smart Ways to Garden on a Budget.* https://modernfarmer.com/2016/02/gardening-ideas-on-a-budget/

Morning Chores & Poindexter, J. (n.d.). *12 Steps to Choosing the Best Location for Your Vegetable Garden.* https://morningchores.com/vegetable-garden-location/

Splan, C. (n.d.). *How Much of a Time Investment per Week Is It to Grow a Vegetable Garden?* SFGATE. https://homeguides.sfgate.com/fall-perennial-planting-65713.html

The Sydney morning herald. (2014, August 14). *The cost of growing your own food.* https://www.smh.com.au/money/saving/the-cost-of-growing-your-own-food-20140814-1045t5.html

Garden Organic. (n.d.). *The No-Dig Method.* https://www.gardenorganic.org.uk/no-dig-method

GrowVeg & Benzinski, K. (2010, November 5). *Planting Systems for Vegetable Gardens.* https://www.growveg.com/guides/planting-systems-for-vegetable-gardens/

Permaculture Research Institute. (n.d.). *What is Permaculture?* https://www.permaculturenews.org/what-is-permaculture/

What Is a Raised Bed, Anyway? (n.d.). Miracle Gro. https://www.miraclegro.com/en-us/library/raised-bed-gardening/what-raised-bed-anyway

Davis, C. P. (2020, July 31). *Organic Foods Guide: When to Buy (or Not Buy) Organic.* On Health. https://www.onhealth.com/content/1/organic_food_nutrition

Food Behind. (n.d.). *Know Some Non-Organic Food Health Risks & Facts.* https://www.foodbehind.com/non-organic-food-health-risks/

Grist & Johnson, N. (2015, November 04). *What does "organic" actually mean?* https://grist.org/food/what-does-organic-actually-mean/

Learn How to Tell When "Organic" on a Label Is True. (2019, January 20). The Balance Small Business. https://www.thebalancesmb.com/when-is-organic-really-organic-2538312

The Optimist & Little, H. (2016, March 31). *Negative effects of non-organic foods.* https://acuoptimist.com/2016/03/negative-effects-of-non-organic-foods/

Organic Growers School. (n.d.). *Why Grow Organic?* https://organicgrowersschool.org/gardeners/library/why-grow-organic/

Red River Basin Commission. (2015, July 22). *The importance of composting.* Manitoba Co-operator. https://www.manitobacooperator.ca/country-crossroads/the-importance-of-composting/

Robinson, L., Segal, J., & Segal, R. (2020, September). *Organic Foods: What You Need to Know.* Help Guide. https://www.helpguide.org/articles/healthy-eating/organic-foods.htm

10 Natural Homemade Organic Fertilizer Recipes. (n.d.). Planet Care Today. https://plantcaretoday.com/natural-organic-fertilizer-recipes.html

Link, R. (2017, May 14). *The 14 Healthiest Vegetables on Earth.* https://www.healthline.com/nutrition/14-healthiest-vegetables-on-earth

SanSone, A. (2021, March 24). *15 Best Vegetables to Grow for Gardeners of Any Skill Level.* The Pioneer woman. https://www.thepioneerwoman.com/home-lifestyle/gardening/g35888049/best-vegetables-to-grow/

Stinchcombe, C. (2020, June 18). *11 Easy-to-Grow Vegetables and Herbs (Especially If You Don't Have a Lot of Space).* Self. https://www.self.com/story/easy-vegetables-herbs-to-grow

Sweetser, R. (2019, January 29). *The healthiest vegetables you can grow in the garden!* The Old Farmer's Almanac. https://www.almanac.com/healthiest-vegetables-you-can-grow-garden#

Better Homes and Gardens. (2020, September 15). *25 Gardening Tips Every Gardener Should Know.* https://www.bhg.com/gardening/yard/garden-care/gardening-tips-for-every-gardener/

Earth's Ally. (n.d.). *How to Effectively Keep Pests Away from an Organic Vegetable Garden.* https://earthsally.com/gardening-basics/how-to-effectively-keep-pests-away-from-an-organic-vegetable-garden.html

Fra-Dor. (2018, October 4). *What is the best mulch for vegetable gardens?* https://frador.com/what-is-the-best-mulch-for-vegetable-gardens/#:~:text=Mulches%20help%20control%20weeds%2C%20prevent,to%20reduce%20foliage%20and%20disease.

Gardener's supply company & LaLiberte, K. (2021, January 25). *When to Water.* https://www.gardeners.com/how-to/when-to-water/8108.html

Kelly, T. (2021, July 1). *Brilliant budget garden ideas – boost your outdoor space without breaking the bank!* Ideal Home. https://www.idealhome.co.uk/garden/garden-ideas/budget-garden-ideas-197528

Ly, L. (n.d.). *6 Simple Tips for Maintaining Your Gardening Tools.* Garden Betty. https://www.gardenbetty.com/6-simple-tips-for-maintaining-your-gardening-tools/

Megan. (n.d.). *Secrets to Watering Your Vegetable Garden the Right Way.* The Creative Vegetable Gardener. https://www.creativevegetablegardener.com/watering-vegetable-garden/

Better Homes and Gardens & Beck, A. (2021, March 19). *Follow This Spring Gardening Checklist for a Gorgeous Landscape Year-Round.* https://www.bhg.com/gardening/yard/garden-care/spring-gardening-checklist/

Blesch, W. (2020, December 11). *How plants detect seasonal changes, and what it means for your garden.* HappySprout. https://www.happysprout.com/inspiration/seasons-plants/

5 Tips for a Flourishing Summer Garden – Help Your Garden Take the Heat. (n.d.). Gardening Cook. https://thegardeningcook.com/5-tips-for-a-flourishing-summer-garden/

Getting Started: Gardening Through the Different Seasons. (n.d.). SeedsNow. https://www.seedsnow.com/pages/getting-started-gardening-through-the-different-seasons

JandJfoods. (n.d.). *List of Peak Seasons for Fruits and Veggie.* http://www.jandjfoods.com/list-of-peak-seasons-for-fruits-and-veggie

LaBarbera, M. (2012, April 12). *Parents' Guide - List of Vegetables by Season.* Nourish Interactive. http://www.nourishinteractive.com/healthy-living/free-nutrition-articles/98-vegetables-by-season

Owen, M. (n.d.). *How to Communicate with Plants.* Plantea. http://www.plantea.com/talk.htm

Southern Living Plant Collection & Toscano, K. (2020, December 28). *5 Ways to Protect Your Garden this Winter.* https://southernlivingplants.com/planting-care/5-ways-to-protect-your-garden-this-winter/

Woodies Garden Goods. (2017, December 5). *The Ultimate Guide to Seasonal Gardening.* https://

gardengoodsdirect.com/blogs/news/ultimate-guide-to-seasonal-gardening

GrowVeg & Bradbury, K. (2010, November 5). *Storing and Preserving Your Garden Harvest*. https://www.growveg.com/guides/storing-and-preserving-your-garden-harvest/

Grundig. (n.d.). *10 Useful tips on how to take care of fruits and vegetables*. https://www.respectfood.com/article/10-useful-tips-on-how-to-take-care-of-fruits-and-vegetables/

Harbour, S. (2021, July 1). *5 vegetable garden harvesting mistakes and how to fix them*. An offgrid Life. https://www.anoffgridlife.com/vegetable-gardening-harvesting-mistakes/

Jake. (2014, September 4). *Why is Rain Such a Problem at Harvest?* A YEAR IN THE LIFE OF A FARMER. https://thelifeofafarmer.com/2014/09/04/why-is-rain-such-a-problem-at-harvest/

Natria. (n.d.). *How To Preserve Excess Produce*. https://www.natria.com/learn/edible-gardening/how-preserve-excess-produce

PennState Extension. (2006, May 12). *Proper Care and Handling of Fruits and Vegetables*. https://extension.psu.

edu/proper-care-and-handling-of-fruits-and-vegetables

Renee's Garden & Formiga, A. (n.d.). *When the Time Is Ripe: Harvesting Vegetables for Best Flavor*. https://www.reneesgarden.com/blogs/gardening-resources/98156289-when-the-time-is-ripe-harvesting-vegetables-for-best-flavor

www.ingramcontent.com/pod-product-compliance
Lightning Source LLC
LaVergne TN
LVHW091308150826
845673LV00006B/1584